Like Water

Like Water

The Extraordinary Approach
to Education at Fairhaven School

By Mark McCaig

Fairhaven School Press
Upper Marlboro, Maryland

Fairhaven School Press
17900 Queen Anne Road
Upper Marlboro, MD 20774
Visit our web site at www.fairhavenschool.com

Second Edition: April 2009

Library of Congress Cataloguing in Publication Data

McCaig, Mark.
Like Water.
Summary: Essays about life at Fairhaven
School, a Sudbury school in rural Maryland.
[Education—Nonfiction]

ISBN 978-0-615-20280-8

Printed in the United States of America
by Fidlar Doubleday Inc.

All poetry is by Mark McCaig unless otherwise indicated.

Cover, book design and editing by Lisa Lyons
Photograph on page 20 by Alice Wells.
All other photographs by Lisa Lyons

for Kim McCaig

Writing this book reminded me time after time of the great debt we at Fairhaven School owe the founders, staff and students of Sudbury Valley School. The blood, sweat and tears of Fairhaven are ours, but the template was set by Sudbury Valley. Thanks also to the founders, staff, and students of Fairhaven School. Fleda Brown provided editing assistance. A special note of gratitude to Lisa Lyons for editing and designing this book.

"Education swirls around us and changes us every moment of every day. There are many ways to describe the experience of a Sudbury school life, and perhaps this is the best one — no matter how serene water sometimes looks, it is in fact constantly changing and moving. All students who have the privilege of attending a Sudbury school know this feeling. Their lives are never still, and their plans for the future never static. They know the power of the surges of energy and motivation. We hope you will understand more about this environment from reading Like Water.*"*

— Mimsy Sadofsky,
a founder of Sudbury Valley School,
co-author of *The Pursuit of Happiness*

Contents

VIII Contents

In September

Out come the orb weavers, a real spider's spider,
their banner homes waving over the breezeway,
connecting post to beam, post to beam.

Do they catch the words walking by?
Do their black and white legs scramble up webs
to reap teenage snippets trapped in the wind-

can't believe JC or *food run* or *capture the flag?*
And what lingers, the lambent afternoon
someone whacks the web with a stick,

beyond the threads, dangling like vowels?
In September, school's back in.
Voices echo from the word factory:

behind the swings, where water falls,
in the nook of a maple branch, a pinpoint spider

spins its whole world, no wider than Sasha's hand,
still enough for sustenance, plenty to hear
wait for me and *to the stream, to the stream.*

Introduction:
A Holy Curiosity

ONE AFTERNOON I ROCKED the glider on the breezeway that connects the two rustic buildings of Fairhaven School. A thirteen-year-old student joined me, and we began discussing the latest Washington Wizards victory in the green glow of hardwood trees. A wood thrush fluted its three notes every few minutes during our conversation, one that touched on philosophy, politics, and the future of the school. Other school members passed, each engaged in their day as fully as we were, taking no special notice of us. For the first of many times, I understood that Fairhaven had become what we'd envisioned years before: a place of beauty and learning, where the remarkable is commonplace.

The most striking natural feature at Fairhaven is the stream that runs along the northern border of campus. From time to time, a log will block the course, attracting leaves and other detritus to further impede the water. Just as we liberate the stream when this occurs, the founders and staff of this school have removed as many obstacles to curiosity as possible. Like water in our clear stream, the passionately curious young people in

Fairhaven School flow freely toward knowledge and adulthood.

How do you describe a pristine stream in a world of dams
and polluted waters? Because Fairhaven's such a dynamic
place, all of us-- parents, students, and staff members-- perceive
Fairhaven in myriad ways. Nevertheless, salient features distinguish the school- a Sudbury school modeled after the Sudbury
Valley School in Framingham, Massachusetts. Below is a summary of the distinctive aspects of Fairhaven School.

Time
Fairhaven students are completely responsible for how they
spend their time. They do what they want, when they want,
provided they follow the democratically-generated school
rules. They seldom seem rushed and can spend hours, weeks
and months on distinct activities- playing the drum kit, climbing trees, perhaps reading the latest Harry Potter.

Governance
The school is a participatory democracy, wherein students share
total access to decision-making. Students and staff vote at the
Judicial Committee once a day, at School Meeting once a week,
and parents, staff and students vote at Assembly meetings three
times a year. School Meeting decides everything, including who
works here, whether to buy a new vacuum cleaner, and what
the safety procedures are for working in the shop.

Age Mixing
Fairhaven's students gather according to their interests and
friendships, not according to their ages. Crossing our campus,

you may see a five-year-old riding piggyback on a teenager or an adult teaching math to a mixed-age class. An older girl may be showing her younger friend a shortcut on the laptop, or a young boy may be charming someone into reading his favorite Dr. Seuss. This departure from the basic grouping strategy in traditional schools enhances the flow of life at Fairhaven.

Learning

We acknowledge that people are always learning, and therefore Fairhaven recognizes the intrinsic value of all educational pursuits. While students sometimes engage in traditional academic classes—they've studied Algebra to Zen—most learning is informal and experiential. Our students learn about their lives by taking charge of them and living them fully. In the relative absence of formal classes, life itself becomes the curriculum.

Play

The most common activity at school is play. Because it's so pervasive, play on campus has as many faces as the people who engage in it: organized games like basketball or Hearts, role playing games like "house," constructing paper dolls, telling jokes, building block cities. Play is the basic learning modality of children everywhere, and our students embrace it.

Freedom

In a world where young people's rights are limited, Fairhaven is an island of freedom. Our students seize it, guard it, respect it, and use it to grow without hindrance into adults. Students have spent entire days hanging out on the porch; they've spent entire days studying mathematics. They choose. Above all else, freedom defines our school.

Responsibility

The genius of the Sudbury Valley School's founders was their recognition that a free school must also expect its students to take responsibility for their decisions. A case in point is graduation. In order to graduate, each Fairhaven candidate must write and defend a thesis explaining how they have prepared themselves to become effective adults in the larger community. For many students, freedom is the easy part. Taking responsibility for their choices, for their lives, at the same time? The hard part.

> *"The important thing is not to stop questioning. Curiosity has its own reasons for existing. One cannot help but be in awe when he contemplates the mysteries of eternity, of life, of the marvelous structure of reality. It is enough if one tries to comprehend a little of this mystery every day. Never lose a holy curiosity."*
>
> — Albert Einstein

A mixture of anecdotes and philosophy, this book provides a guided tour of the practices and potential of a Fairhaven School education, and of Fairhaven School itself, a place established so that its young people will never lose a "holy curiosity."

The Beating Heart
of the School

*Order without liberty and liberty without order
are equally destructive.*

—Theodore Roosevelt

PRAYING MANTISES ABOUND on campus in November. Big ones.
One year students took to feeding them live crickets, staring
rapt as the enormous bugs consumed the crickets like people
chew corn on the cob. Soon they attempted to stage a fight between two mantises, and word of this reached the animal rights
maven of the school. By filling out a grievance form about the
incident, she hauled them into the Judicial Committee (JC),
claiming, "It upset my right to exist peaceably, it's cruelty to
animals, and it's just plain wrong."

Called into JC, the younger boys stared like the hapless

crickets before her allegations. Others, however, took up their cause. "I find it ironic that this complaint comes from the head of the Snake Corporation. Don't you feed the garter snakes live goldfish?" asked one JC member.

"Yes, but the goldfish are bred for food. They were going to die anyway," she countered.

"Aren't the mantises going to die anyway?" the JC member pressed on. JC then discovered from witnesses that neither mantis was injured in their brief skirmish. How is it cruelty to animals if no animal got hurt?

The plaintiff testified, "Well, I hear one of the mantises tried to get away and they forced it to come back and fight." JC confirmed the fact; the organizers had done so. "This hurt the mantis's feelings. It's just as cruel."

A teenager who was watching the proceedings shot his hand up. "It's a bug! It doesn't have an autonomic nerve system. It doesn't have feelings."

The complainant pulled her legs to her chest and rocked slightly, undeterred. "I know they have feelings, and this brutality hurt their feelings."

JC debated the case for a few minutes, finally voting by a three-to-two margin to charge the bug fight organizer with cruelty to animals. One member abstained from voting. After obtaining the boy's plea of "No Contest," JC voted to sentence him to ten minutes cleaning the grounds. Onlookers to the fight were not charged, despite attempts to charge them with our bedrock "Preamble"[1] rule because they did not stop the alleged barbarity. They were informally warned. No one brought a complaint against the Snake Corporation.

Thus the case entered the records, joining other allegations of cruelty to animals like the time students were stomping ants (charged) and the time a student killed a black widow spider (not charged.) In our first year we had a mild mouse problem and I advised a fellow staff member to freeze a captured rodent, on the theory that it would be a painless death. Indignant students brought her into JC, where she said she was just doing her job, keeping the school clean. The students opined that the snap of a mousetrap was faster and thereby less cruel than slow death by freezing. I was brought in as the mastermind. After JC voted not to charge either of us, the complainants wrote legislation prohibiting cruelty to animals, bringing it to School Meeting for swift passage.

Chartered and overseen by School Meeting and convening every day, the Judicial Committee is the most important and the most active committee or corporation at the school. At once practical and fascinating, the JC may be Sudbury Valley's greatest invention. It is where the rubber meets the road, where the freedom and responsibility intersect, collide, and coexist. In many ways, the JC is the beating heart of the school. As one student said, "Without JC, this place would fall apart."

Aside from School Meeting, only the JC may interrupt any activity and demand a School Meeting member's immediate presence. *West Side Story* rehearsal? Working on next year's budget with the Bookkeeping Committee? Playing house with your friends, and you're the dog? We all must drop what we're doing to come to JC, whether we're plaintiff, defendant or witness. What is this body, and why has a fiercely independent community succumbed to its will these ten years?

Fairhaven's very first School Meeting chartered the Judicial Committee, and it has been meeting daily to settle grievances ever since. Every School Meeting member must serve on JC as assigned by the Law Clerk, the person annually elected by School Meeting to oversee the JC. The Law Clerk divides the

School Meeting membership into five age groups and assigns a person from each group to JC. At Fairhaven, a term lasts two weeks. When the school had lower enrollment, students had to serve multiple terms on JC over the course of the year; one term per year is typical these days. Bear in mind that the weekly School Meeting has enacted all of the rules and practices concerning JC. Innovations continue.

Every six weeks, School Meeting also elects JC Clerks and Alternate Clerks. Whereas the Law Clerk maintains the Lawbook and the judicial database, and monitors the smooth functioning of the system, the JC Clerks run the daily meetings. Becoming a successful JC Clerk takes patience, communication skills, persistence, and grit. Meetings average between one and two hours every day, and the clerks are the daily face of order at Fairhaven. Negotiating college or the labor market may seem easy compared to clerking your umpteenth mess-in-the-Chesapeake-Room case with a half-dozen or so students.

The judicial process at Fairhaven is egalitarian to the core. Anybody can allege rule-breaking by completing a write-up form about the incident. Staff members and fellow students assist students who are not proficient writers. Some students delight in writing up staff members. When accused, staff members too must come to the JC and answer questions.

Sometimes students who target staff for trivial write-ups become acquainted with the concept of payback by ending up charged themselves for breaking a rule. One day I was talking to an alumnus on the breezeway, twirling a small stick. A teenager ran by, clapping me extra hard on the back. I flicked the stick at him. He removed his headphones with much indignity, saying, "I'm writing you up!"

The graduate cautioned, "You're writing him up? You just smacked his back!" The current student wrote me up. When the

JC met the next day, they voted to charge us both with the "right to exist peaceably rule."[2] We both received warnings.

Coming to JC for the first time is daunting for both young and old. Picture a table surrounded by the Committee members, with the Clerks facing you. A pile of grievances and the red three-ring binder containing the Lawbook rest on the table. Onlookers usually people the room. For a new, young student the setting can feel intimidating. One girl spent an entire year whispering testimony to her very un-shy friend who relayed it, verbatim, to the JC, happy to accommodate her.

While it may look at first like the Principal's Office, these new students learn that it does not at all feel like the principal's office. As at all Sudbury schools, the judicial process is absolute in its commitment to due process. Deliberation is public and open. JC calls witnesses and writes, then adopts by vote a detailed report of what happened.

Though they seldom have, defendants can "plead the Fifth" and elect not to incriminate themselves. They also have the option of pleading not guilty when charged with breaking a rule. In these rare cases, the defendant pleads her case to the next School Meeting. Defendants who do not wish to challenge the finding may plead no contest and accept JC's sentence. Defendants and other School Meeting members may also appeal to School Meeting if they disagree with a JC decision.

The final piece of each case resulting in a charge is sentencing. Sentences usually call for restrictions, community service, or reparations. The most common JC cases are violations of the following rule: "1-30-10. Everyone is responsible for cleaning up after themselves." Typical JC sentences for not cleaning up (or in JC parlance "leaving a mess") are cleaning part of the school or restricting people from the room where the mess occurred. Serial mess-makers incur more aggressive sentences, such as a restriction to eating only at a certain table for the next month.

In JC, if you break it, you buy it. So pleading guilty to a charge of violating rule 1-20-10 in the Lawbook—destruction, alteration, or misuse of school property—means you have to repair or pay for what you destroyed, altered or misused. Break a window? Pay for its replacement. Doodle on a picnic table? Sand it. Misuse the glue gun? You lose the privilege to use it. Whenever possible, JC votes for sentences that are logical and reasonable.

Free people, especially free children, like to run; but other free people, including children, want an orderly, safe school, one that is not disrupted by runners. JC often got creative, in our first decade, when it came to sentencing violators of the rule prohibiting running in the building. While first-time offenders usually received a warning, early JCs experimented with sentencing repeat offenders to walking in slow motion through the building. Once a JC sentenced a runner to crawl. Although the defendant thought it would have been fun, School Meeting overrode the sentence, invoking its legislation prohibiting cruel and unusual punishment. JCs have restricted runners from rooms, halls, and weather permitting, entire buildings. Recent JCs have, with some success, restricted runners from using any external doors that open into tempting hallways.

The Judicial Committee has its finger on the pulse of the school. If there has been an outbreak of running, the JC must innovate. If the Committee sees the same individual over and over, it must work with that person, perhaps discuss referring the student to School Meeting. Often JC Clerks will propose a new rule or amend an old one at School Meeting resulting from JC business. For example, to accommodate musicians as well as the need for relative quiet, JC Clerks proposed a two-hour window during which loud music may be played.

Each week the Chairman reads to School Meeting the JC Report, a complete, case-by-case listing of the Committee's work from the previous week. This affords School Meeting members the chance to review and oversee the Committee. Reviewing the JC Report often reveals at least one or two cases that need further work. Given its case load, the JC needs the weekly support School Meeting provides. In its wisdom, the School Meeting may find that a young girl was not guilty of the no running rule, or that another student's week-long restriction from the computer room was too severe. Sometimes the review will edit the language of a JC Report.

Attending to the many variables at work in each case—personalities, legal precedent, current events at school, due process—is what makes the Judicial Committee such a profoundly educational system. Maneuvering through each case requires interviewing the principals, synthesizing the facts into a written report, identifying rules that may have been broken, and deciding upon a reasonable consequence. All in a democratic, group setting.

A successful JC buttresses its judicial tasks with compassion and decency. Clerks assess defendants. Are they very young? Are they new to Fairhaven's freedom and responsibility? Are they veteran students, struggling with a new chapter in their lives? Is there a long-standing interpersonal dispute between principals in a case? These and a hundred other factors affect the proceedings. While JC must charge and sentence, the Clerks and Committee members must also retain their humanity by remaining aware of extenuating circumstances.

JC fosters in our students an ongoing awareness of others and a process for maintaining order in a community they value. Years of participation breed in each student an ethical sensibility, a sense of ownership. Some students and staff at first experience the Judicial Committee as an all or nothing process: winners get their cases dropped, losers get charged. Experience often promotes a more sophisticated understanding that recognizes the interplay between the winner/loser surface and the evolving judicial process beneath the surface.

JC might see the same defendant over and over for not eating at a table. For most cases, the Committee has enough evidence to charge and sentence her. On a few occasions, JC decides otherwise. Perhaps no witnesses other than the complainant saw her. Maybe she actually did not violate the rule. In erring on the side of the defendant's innocence until proven guilty, has the JC caused the person who wrote the grievance to "lose?"

Maintaining a system of law and order cannot be reduced to winners and losers; it's an organic process. One day, the repeat offender stops violating the may-only-eat-at-tables rule. Was it because of her punishments? Maybe. Was it because of the number of times she was brought before the Committee by School Meeting members of all stripes for violating the rule? Maybe again. Was it even because of the one or two times there was not enough evidence so she was not charged, even though she broke the rule? Both the student's development and the effect of JC on that development have timetables all their own.

The deliberate and precious fairness of the judicial system at Fairhaven removes every student's feelings of fear or intimidation, sometimes with remarkable speed. They buy in. A nervous student soon breezes into the JC room, assumes responsibility for her actions, signs the form, and goes about her business, hopefully this time running to her next activity *after* she goes outside.

The Judicial Committee concretizes the value the school places on honesty and justice. Sudbury schools stand almost alone as places students are expected to not lie, even by other students, and liars are not admired when they do. One year a new teenager repeatedly denied smoking cigarettes in the woods until eyewitnesses testified that she had. Only then did she admit to smoking. An eight-year-old boy, a Fairhaven veteran who was serving on JC for the multi-day investigation, spoke to JC about the teenager: "Right now I'm thinking that almost anyone is more trustworthy in this school than her."

School Meeting members have also had long, intense discussions about the gap between the no snitching teen culture and the primacy of honor at Fairhaven. An early teen entered the pantheon of student honor when she convinced fellow students to turn themselves in for smoking on campus, an act of contrition and honesty which saved them from expulsion.

There are only a handful of deal-breakers regarding a student's continued enrollment at Fairhaven —ongoing or severe dangerous activity (for example anything to do with fire), illegal activity, perhaps intense anti-social behavior (such as a pattern of acts of violence). Such occurrences and patterns have been quite rare.

Inability or unwillingness to participate in JC is another deal-breaker. Persons found to be lying to JC, not doing sentences, or in any other way obstructing the judicial proceedings are found to be in contempt of JC, a serious offense that usually earns a referral to School Meeting for sentencing. Serial charges of contempt of JC (acting inappropriately during JC) also leads to referrals to School Meeting, suspensions, and discussions of viability at Fairhaven. People must be willing, honest participants in the JC process at school, or they cannot come. It is that central.

Participating in JC teaches people the basic premise of civil society: there are agreed upon rules that must be followed, and not following them has consequences for the individual and the society. Yet JC is seldom cut and dried. Each case has its nuances.

Was anybody else part of this mess? Has the defendant left other messes?

"I was running in the building, but he was chasing me."

Is the Clerk having a bad day? Has the JC been cracking down on running in the building lately? Was the defendant angry when he hit him?

"Yes I called her that, but it was a joke."

"Well, I didn't think it was funny. It insulted me." Was it a sexist remark?

And a JC that's cruising along, handing out parking tickets if you will, will suddenly brake for a significant conversation. We discuss the line between humor and sexism, the rights and limits of free speech, the nature of liberty itself. The Judicial Committee is simultaneously practical and deep, maintaining the school's order and debating philosophical issues. Schools and publishers that spend untold millions attempting to develop critical thinking in young people need only establish JCs. It's almost impossible to come into JC and not think. Issues and discussions tend to linger in the mind long after a case is closed. A case in point—those poor praying mantises and their hurt feelings.

Astronomy:
How the School Works

Two teenagers approached me one day in the Old Building. "I hear you know something about astronomy," Kelly said.

"I know a thing or two. Mostly self-taught," I replied. "You interested?"

"Yeah, Mark. We want to learn about stars," said Barbara, laughing. The inside joke was Barbara's rep as the school's celebrity fanatic, a walking tabloid. She had been working a Cher look all year.

"I'd love to do a class, maybe do a lab with telescopes at night. Put up a sign-up sheet to see who's interested. Get back to me in a week," I said.

Astronomy. One of my passions, it's a subject that seems to have universal interest. Most years at school, somebody asks me about it. I've had many conversations with students about eclipses and meteor showers, Venus and galaxies. The perihelion of Mars in 2003, when the red planet was closer to earth than it had been in 60,000 years, fostered queries. But never a class.

The girls posted the sign-up sheet in the stairwell between the notices for a field trip to the Baltimore Zoo and a dance class. Three others signed up over the course of the week. The girls returned, sheet in hand. They were serious.

We arranged to meet once a week. I prepared for the first few classes, wrote a syllabus. We would start with the solar system, then move outward. I brought in a telescope with a solar filter. We looked at sunspots, then returned to the classroom and began an overview of the planets. We ended the first day by arranging our first nocturnal telescope lab, weather permitting.

Unfettered by the suburban light pollution of their own neighbor-

hoods, the students and I beheld the winter sky. Kelly peered into the telescope. "Don't look directly at the nebula, and it will be clearer. It's called averting your eyes," I said.

"Yeah, I see it," Kelly said. "Cool." She looked a few seconds more, then backed away. Her eyes found the fuzzy patch, the nebula without the scope.

"M42 is one of the 103 deep sky objects catalogued by Charles Messier. It's called the Orion nebula." I was adjusting the telescope, compensating for the earth's rotation. "Astronomers think there's a new star forming right there in the middle."

"Are we going to look at all hundred and three tonight?" asked Barbara. Her slim, silver down coat was ultra-hip, but low on function. We'd been at it forty-five minutes. I wondered if Cher enjoyed astronomy. Barbara swept the sky with binoculars. "Hey Mark, what's that?"

A satellite was slipping by. In a lifetime of observing, I had seen them increase ten-fold. "That's how your cell phone works. It's a satellite," I told her. She followed it until it disappeared above the horizon.

I pointed out how much the Pleiades cluster had moved since we first scoped it. "Should we call it a night?" I asked. Most folks have about an hour of astronomy lab in them. I didn't want these new eyes to go super nova.

"Definitely," said Barbara. "I mean, it's cool and all, but my feet are freezing." She was the first person who'd used my telescope in heels. She flipped open her cell, calling her mom to pick her up.

The next week back at school, only Kelly showed up for class. I folded my binder.

"What's the deal?" I asked her, bothered. "Did I spend too much time talking the other night?"

"That was awesome. We all liked it, even Barbara."

"But nobody's here for class."

Kelly thought for a second. She worked part-time in the office at this point, and would do so full time after graduating for a couple years before moving to Arizona for college. She understood the school.

"Look, Mark, you didn't do anything wrong. The class was fine. Looking through the telescope was amazing. People just moved on to other things. That's how the school works."

This time I thought for a while. Kelly waited. "You mean you guys just wanted to see what astronomy's like? Like a sample?" Not understand the whole universe, I heard myself thinking.

"Exactly," she said. "I like that. We were sampling."

Catching Lightning in a Bottle

Don't try to start a school. It's too hard. Just
move near one that's already up and running.

—Mimsy Sadofsky

AFTER 40 REWARDING BUT CHALLENGING YEARS at Sudbury
Valley, Mimsy often offers this as her first piece of advice to
people wanting to start their own Sudbury school. Of course,
when people persevere she offers her unstinting support, but
having created the Sudbury school and having seen the
Sisyphean struggles of Sudbury startup groups worldwide,
she's blunt with newcomers. Herewith is a brief history of
founding Fairhaven School, a five-year process that involved so
many people and such hard work, good timing, resources and
luck that it exemplifies baseball legend Leo Durocher's remark
about catching lightning in a bottle. It was exactly like that. But
somehow we did.

Why We Went After that Lightning

For many of Fairhaven's founders, the desire to create a better kind of school began with our own quite varied school experiences. I, for example, attended St. Theresa of the Little Flower School, a parochial school operated by nuns. Like the other founders, I was trying to understand the shortcomings of my own education and create a school for young people in Maryland that avoided those shortcomings. Our adult experiences teaching in conventional schools or raising our own children reinforced the questions we were raising about learning and growing. We all began to conclude that there had to be a better way.

For many of us A.S. Neill's *Summerhill*, a book about the famed British free school, was an eye opener. Neill founded Summerhill with the belief that "the function of a child is to live his own life — not the life that his anxious parents think he should live, not a life according to the purpose of an educator who thinks he knows best."[1] Kim McCaig, my wife and co-founder, in particular, retained her admiration for Summerhill and its radical approach despite her education professor's dismissal of free schooling as an idea that had run its course.

Beginnings

After abandoning conventional teaching careers, Kim and I began teaching nearby homeschooling families an experiential science curriculum. Living at the beach with access to birds, fossils, trees, and the Bay itself, we wrote a curriculum with lots of outside time and projects.

I had learned about Sudbury Valley School from a classmate in graduate school. Towards the end of our first year working at home, we ordered Sudbury Valley's startup kit for school founders. After devouring its contents, we were hooked. We phoned a neighbor who joined. It was 1993. We crafted a one-page proposal for a second year working with the homeschoolers, spending most of our energy on one sentence towards the middle of the page. Although the document is long gone, the gist was that we would prepare and offer another directed science curriculum, but the students would be free to choose whether they participated in the activities or not. Agreeing to three days per week and a modest fee, the parents sent us twelve children aged five to eleven for the real first year of what would become Fairhaven School.

Although we dissected frogs that year, the directed science curriculum didn't stand a chance. Two students listened to a Counting Crows CD with guitars in hand, playing songs over and over to learn the chords. People baked in the kitchen. Some played the board game Parcheesi for untold hours. Interesting adults came, adding to the mix of activity. Students collected sharks' teeth and made daisy crowns. They hung out. We established a judicial committee for dealing with problems, and we agreed upon rules.

Over the next five years, an annual school co-op met regularly, attracting not only the initial families, who had chosen homeschooling for reasons unrelated to the Sudbury concept, but also new families who wanted educational freedom for their children. They read the Sudbury materials, notably Daniel Greenberg's *Free at Last*.[2] Joining the original students two or three days per week gave these new students somewhere to play Legos, write stories, and create dance routines.

These co-op students and staff began establishing Fairhaven's school culture, that invisible ethos that characterizes every school, Sudbury or not. Meeting first at a beach community, then at a former sharecropper's house on a large farm strengthened our commitment to an interesting natural setting with major access to the outdoors. Many aspects of Fairhaven's culture—shared stories, particular games, and a service orientation—trace their roots to the early years.

Who would staff Fairhaven School? The co-ops were a multi-year crash course in Sudbury school staffing. Many of us with experience in traditional, curriculum-driven schools had as much to un-learn as we had to learn. Working with the early batches of students became a process of letting go of adult control and embracing trust in human nature that staff members and parents continue today. The current staff dialogue about working in a Sudbury school began during the first days of the co-op. Would you write that mess up or give the student a warning? What do you do if students don't show up for a class? The co-ops provided crucial job experience to learn from and discuss.

Soon after a kitchen table meeting that voted unanimously to start a school, we began meeting as school founders, creating a meeting record and another culture that continues to the present. Because some of the initial people resided on the western shore of the Chesapeake Bay in a town called Fairhaven, an early founders meeting voted to name the school-to-be Fairhaven School. Not merely a geographic choice, the name's elements worked: "fair" captured the school's commitment to student rights and egalitarianism, while we saw ourselves as a "haven" from traditional schooling.

Like other Sudbury school startups, the Fairhaven School founders meetings were democratic. For most of us, they represented our first encounter with participatory democracy. By the time we opened, we had several School Meeting and Assembly members with considerable experience in democratic decision-making.

We scheduled a series of informational meetings at the nearby public library just up the coast from Fairhaven in Deale. One event featured Mimsy's son Hal Sadofsky, a Sudbury Valley School graduate who would later co-found the Blue Mountain School in Oregon. He lived in Baltimore then and gave our abstract description of the proposed school some much-needed flesh and blood. Ken Pruitt, another SVS alumnus who lived nearby, offered his insight and experience to the Fairhaven founders. To this day, some of our best PR has come from real live encounters with actual students and graduates both from Fairhaven and other Sudbury schools.

Becoming Legitimate

As a groundswell of interest grew, founding the school soon became a process involving numerous parallel tracks: developing a corporate structure, meeting as a co-op, hosting public relations events, educating ourselves, networking with Sudbury schools, fundraising, and perhaps most significant of all, finding a home for the school. Rather than bounce from home to home as an informal cooperative, we decided early in the process to seek approval from the Maryland State Board of Education to become a real school. We wanted to be legitimate, and we set ourselves to the task.

In a process similar to writing the proposal to give freedom to the first batch of homeschoolers, founders prepared our application for the State Board of Education. We included Sudbury Valley books, our credentials as teachers, and a carefully worded letter about the school. We told the Board how many Maryland families wanted this school for their children. Founders agonized over the packet. Which SVS books should we include? Is this paragraph too pushy? Does the letter take shots at public education?

From the outset, we had made a conscious decision to not

criticize traditional schools as part of our public relations strategy. Of course the overarching influence of the system and the experiences both of the founders and of our listening audiences made comparisons inevitable. Several of us had taught in traditional schools, both public and private. Still, Fairhaven's founders committed to focusing, whenever possible, on the positives of Sudbury schooling rather than what we perceived as the negative aspects of traditional schooling. This remains a fundamental principle of our Public Relations Committee, and it has served us well. The compulsory school systems speak for themselves, and people who do not feel like their educational choices are under attack are more open to considering a different approach.

We met the Board's non-public schools supervisor in Baltimore a few weeks after we sent our application. It soon became clear that she was not familiar with the materials we had sent. Undaunted, we pitched the Sudbury concept vis-à-vis Fairhaven School in an hour-long meeting. We presented Sudbury Valley's extensive data on its graduates. Surely, we told one another in the elevator ride following the meeting, she would grant us state recognition as an independent school. Back home, we hung up our fancy clothes and got back to the dozens of other tasks at hand.

In the literary world rejection letters are notoriously thin; at least ours was three pages long. "The state of Maryland requires a sequential and linear curriculum, including the following specific courses..." The language deviated from boilerplate to acknowledge our interesting ideas and the state's support of innovation, but reminded us that innovation must occur within the framework outlined above. Then, in the last paragraph, a light at the end of the tunnel: if we insisted on continuing with our school project, the only way to do it in the state of Maryland would be to become a church-sponsored school. It turns out that church-sponsored schools are not subject to any curriculum oversight by the State Board in Maryland.

The founders' commitment to Sudbury schooling was unstinting. In describing the importance of educational freedom being absolute, SVS founder and writer Daniel Greenberg put it this way: "You can't be a little bit pregnant." By the time we received the state Board's letter, the proverbial rabbit had been long dead. Fairhaven School students would have educational freedom; we were going to be a Sudbury school or nothing.

Our attorney confirmed the long tradition separating church and state in Maryland, a tradition with roots in Maryland's colonial history as a haven for Roman Catholics in a newly Protestant land. Some founders who had already been gathering monthly to meditate and explore spiritual matters incorporated as Cherry Hill Meeting, becoming a bona fide church in the state. The Meeting elected officers and adopted a one-page creed supporting the right of each individual to pursue his or her own path of growth and development.[3] Renamed the Fairhaven Community Fellowship many years ago, the church has been meeting and sponsoring Fairhaven School ever since. While the school buildings are compliant with all school building codes and regulations, and the employees undergo background checks, as a church school we are blessedly free from the state's curriculum mandates.

In 1996, founders attended the second professional conference at Sudbury Valley School for schools and startup groups. Over the years, these workshops have provided essential support, networking, and training. Exposure to experienced staff and founders from sister schools softened the Fairhaven founders' collective learning curve. Ideas percolated; connections were established. Growing out of one set of these connections, the Red Cedar School, a Sudbury school in Vermont, hired me as a staff member for one year. Wanting more experience than the part-time cooperatives could offer, I spent a year working in an established Sudbury environment, learning from its staff and students, from its School Meeting and Assembly.

The Fellowship is a democratically governed church that holds business meetings quarterly at the school. It has evolved a sub-structure of activities similar to the school's, wherein Fellowship members who share an interest form study groups and meet. Sanctioned study groups have formed around a variety of subjects, among them dance, poetry, drumming, yoga, a women's group, a book group, and a community service group. Just like at school, interests fluctuate. The Fellowship charters new study groups each year, and inactive groups disband.

Although we are in fact a church-sponsored institution, we do not provide religious instruction per se. Some years ago students requested a comparative religions course, and conversations about religion abound on campus. We have enrolled families with many different religious beliefs. Many families keep their religious beliefs private. Both the school and the Fellowship expressly tolerate all religious influences.

Finding a Site
A handful of charismatic, energized people joined the group and kicked it into another gear entirely. Infusion of new blood attracted new people, new ideas and new energy to the biggest hurdle, finding a physical home for the school.

Our search for potential school sites ran the gamut, from abandoned schools to homes for sale, from empty commercial properties to one historic but failing restaurant. The group landed for one year in a church basement as the Crossroads Cooperative. Some founders just drove up and down Anne

Arundel County, searching for possible locations. Zoning classifications restricted many sites. Building codes necessitated significant renovations to everything we considered.

Meanwhile, the critical mass of families grew, but still we had no site. Finally, founder Romey Pittman's husband Sam Droege threw down the gauntlet. They had two children soon to be school age. They had recently built their own log cabin. "Are you going to open this school or what? Why don't you just build it?" Never one to turn down a challenge, Romey turned the corner, convincing the founders to purchase the magnificent hilltop seven acres with a stream we now know as the campus. Founders with the means and the willingness to do so leveraged personal assets to secure the first mortgage. Acquiring the site added instant credibility, attracting more founders and students. The Co-op took regular field trips to the tranquil site. The young people enacted their freedom on campus.

The summer of 1998 was one of the hottest and driest to date in the state of Maryland. By then, we were not going to let anything like heat waves or droughts prevent us from opening, on time, in September, 1998.

Construction!
Building what we now call "the old building" attracted volunteers for a number of reasons. The founders and builders adopted an environmental ethic for the project, to save money and maximize efficiency as well as out of conviction. Sam milled the timbers that frame the building on site or at their nearby farm. We joined a network of green builders, actually deconstructing homes slated for demolition in order to salvage materials, including one NBA star's mansion. His windows and glass doors still shed light into the Shop and the Art Room. Many of the two-by-fours that support the walls in the

old building used to support other walls, and volunteers spent hours de-nailing them. BP Solar donated photovoltaic panels as part of its solar schools program. Many people helped build the school because of the founders' pervasive "green" commitment.

Others joined the effort because they wanted a Sudbury school in Maryland, mostly for their own children. Scores of people pounded nails, hung drywall, and painted. Alan White, a board member and founder of Sudbury Valley, and a contractor with extensive construction experience, volunteered his labor for the entire summer. We hired two other contractors and paid some professionals (plumbers, septic field experts, an architect), but the vast majority of the labor that built the first building was voluntary. Parents of the initial batch of students included a plumber, a drywall hanger, a carpenter, and an electrician.

A group called the DC Single Volunteers adopted our project, sending industrious folks our way every weekend. One stalwart member of this group who happened to be between jobs volunteered full time for the entire three months.

These and others were attracted to both the natural beauty of the campus and to the contagious excitement of the founders. As with all building projects, crises came and went. Still, we persevered. Raising the timbers felt just like a barn-raising must have felt in earlier communities. We opened the school in the brand new building with thirty-three students on September 23, 1998, only one day later than our goal.

In the lifecycle of non-profit organizations, nothing quite matches the excitement or the drama of the beginning. Fairhaven now has twelve acres and two buildings. There's talk of building a third. We're well into the subsequent phase of maintaining the school. Still, the passion and zeal of those first years —especially the summer of 1998—permeate the rustic old building, our ongoing testament to what is possible against the odds. Somewhere in a closet, perhaps under a couch, the lightning we managed to catch still flickers in a thick bottle, ever attracting students to its magnetic glow.

The Importance
of Talking Trash

"It's the bottom of the 12th, with Manny on first. Quantrill's pitch." Pause. "Oh, this Fenway crowd knows he got all of that one! It's gone!" Mock crowd noise. "With their backs to the wall, the Sox have done it. They're still alive." Niel had just entered my grammar class, wearing his shiny, red Boston Red Sox jacket.

Johnny shook his head, doffed his Yankees cap, sportsman-like. "Yeah, you guys won last night, but we're still up 3-1. The last two games are at The Stadium, and you've got no chance." He was opening his notebook, pulling out last night's homework. Niel joined Johnny and the other three students at his usual spot at the corner of the table.

"Hey, Mark, aren't we doing prepositional phrases today? Like 'over the fence?' asked Niel. "In a sentence: Big Papi hit the ball over the fence." His buddy Pete reached his palm over for some skin.

"I've got a sentence," Johnny came back. "The Red Sox have not won the World Series since 1918. The Yankees haven't won, like, thirty." He was our Achilles, dragging the body of Hector from his chariot.

"I've got a quote on the white board for today's writing prompt, but those of you who seem to have things to say may write about last night's game," I said, closing the door.

It was October, 2004, the year the Red Sox came back from a three games to zero deficit against their archrival Yankees to earn a trip to the World Series that they actually won. My morning grammar and writing class became a box seat as Johnny's Yankee swagger sweated in the daily heat of Niel's Red Sox pluck.

"It's still 3 to 3. No way do we lose at Yankee Stadium again,"

Johnny puffed his chest one more time a few days later, way less New York than he'd been at 3 to 1. The implosion was full-on by now. Poor Johnny was awash in his public lesson on hubris.

"With Kevin Brown pitching? No way. You know it's ovah," Niel crowed, his idea of a Boston accent dragging the last word.

"Can we please go over the homework?" Aisha asked, beyond fed up with these two fanatics. She didn't follow sports, but she knew her grammar. We got to work. They had all signed up for the class, and would continue writing essays and working through a grammar textbook until winter break, well into football season.

The Red Sox completed their historic comeback, beating New York 10 to 3 in the Bronx. We all came to class amazed, maybe feeling a bit sorry for Johnny, even Aisha. Not so Niel, who laid it on way too thick. Johnny snapped, writing Niel up. JC called me as a witness the next day.

"Well, Niel was a bit over the top with Johnny," I began. "But I guess my opinion, since you asked, is that all's fair in love and sports trash talking. Johnny was probably just as harsh with Niel when the Yankees were up 3 to 0. What are you thinking about charging Niel with?"

"Right to exist peaceably," replied the student clerk, no sports fan herself. "Any more questions for Mark?" She looked around the mute JC table. "You can go."

I left. Later I saw Niel, who was agitated. "What's up?" I asked.

"JC freakin' charged me. I can't wear my Sox hat for a day."

"Harsh. Are you going to appeal?"

"I thought about it." He stared into the woods for a long minute, resplendent in his satin Sox jacket. "Nah. We're still in the Series and this time the sorry Yankees are going home. I can go a day without wearing the damn hat."

Ten Years
A Stream of Consciousness

When the school's neighbor who owns the soybean field across the stream told me a nudist colony used to occupy this hilltop campus, I thought, of course it did. Freedom runs deep here at Fairhaven—nowadays people can go barefoot, but not naked; people can talk about sex and drugs and rock and roll, but not do them; well, except for the rock and roll, and I'm cool with that, just ask Robert, or Matt, but some days I feel like Uncle Billy in It's a Wonderful Life, *and I've dropped the 8 grand in mean old Mr. Potter's lap and he's just waiting for the bank run to shut us down, then five o'clock rolls around and we're still here, and little Sunshine and I have just buried her dragonfly after trying to revive it in the sun, and she's asked it to say hello to her cat Lucky, in heaven, and aside from the dragonfly, at day's end nobody's hurt—well, not too bad—and nobody's sued us, and they all do learn to read, and much more, and actually, our students are ethical, bright, shining gifts to the world, just talk to them, because now they're coming back to visit as grown-ups, with shoes on their feet, though they might kick them off when they're here, and like I said, it's five o'clock and my colleagues and I are dancing around the office like George Bailey and Uncle Billy after the bank run and we're holding up our two dollar bills and kissing them cause we're still open, dammit, and the next morning we'll be here and the morning after that and the morning after that and now I'm unlocking the door and it hits me that it's been ten years of dollar bill dances and pristine openings just like the very first morning, ten years of holding miracle water in our hands, water that never disappears, cool water that's clear but if you drink you taste the clay and the greensand, you taste the salt and maybe just the slightest hint, I swear to you, of chocolate.*

    So I'm leaning on a porch rail explaining to Ricky that only dictators erect solid gold statues to themselves, therefore, no, I won't be supporting his motion at School Meeting, when I smell the sugar cookies baking and two girls run by saying the Kitchen Corp's taking IOUs and lord almighty what's that sound? It's the echo of billions footsteps taken in liberty, and I know it's over a billion because Diana has counted hers today and she pokes her head out from the back seat of the red coupe on the way home and says one thousand, five hundred sixty-seven, and I know we'll extrapolate Monday. That's when I decide, Sunshine, that the ghost of Lucky the cat must sometimes leave heaven to join the ghosts of nudists prowling this very campus, that Lucky must rub up against our legs, keeping us open these ten years, and it has never mattered what they do, just that they do it, from Alex's juggling to Chloe's drumming, and you've never seen people who stand so straight up, so true, as these students, never perfect, always perfectly who they are, and that, my friends, is what I'm talking about, this is what we're celebrating, this little haven of big ideas, this is what I appreciate, all of you who've trusted us, who have trusted your children, all you students who have believed in yourselves, you barefooters who will soon commence your tenth season of chasing windblown leaves, yellow and red, who create for me all these days of wide-eyed amazement, and yes, rock and roll, who spark these incandescent mornings, you brave pioneers who have given me this daily buzz of ten thousand dragonfly moments.

Who's the Boss?

There's a lot of wisdom in this room right here.

—Ernie Marconi, Fairhaven alum

LITTLE ALEXANDER sat in the Chesapeake Room in the folding chair beside me, very cute in his favorite banana yellow Brasil soccer jersey. He had brought a motion to the floor near the end of School Meeting. "I think we should open the rope swing because it's really fun. " He thought a second. "But sometimes you get scratches." Last year's School Meeting had closed the swing for safety concerns.

Leo, the new Grounds Clerk, raised his hand, saying, "That swing is way too dangerous. If you go too far one way, you run into a holly tree. If you miss the holly tree, you might hit a giant tree trunk. Somebody's going to get hurt one day. Putting it there was a bad idea."

School Meeting—it's the boss, it's the headmaster, it's the principal. Every Wednesday at one o'clock, it's where the action is at Fairhaven.

Chloe, the School Meeting Chair, spoke next: "But pushing off the tree trunk is the most fun. That's all I want to say."

Lisa was next, a staff member known for her diplomacy: "I can see how much fun it must be to push off the trunk at the top of your swing. It's always been very important here for students to be able to challenge themselves in exciting, physical ways. However, the current swing placement does seem dangerous."

Alexander fidgeted.

Chloe called on me. "I'm going to give you the back story on the swing," I said. Somebody groaned. "It won't take too long, and it's exciting, involving destruction, danger, even possible death. We've had a rope swing here on and off since before we opened. Somebody put one up on the beech tree by the old building so the kids could play while we built the first building. They turned one of those giant wooden cable spools on its side like a table, then they rigged a ladder behind it so you could jump onto the red boat buoy swing. One day the first year I was in the old office and a huge windstorm blew up. After a few minutes, I heard a terrible crashing sound. I ran outside to see this giant oak tree had fallen directly onto the swing. Now students were on that thing all the time, so I had to check and make sure, you know, that nobody was under that tree."

I paused, just a half beat. "Well, nobody was. That's when we began budgeting for the annual tree trimming. The next site was behind the seesaws, you know where the hill gets super steep? One day I went back to the swing to see none other than our own Joey Johnson hanging upside down, swinging, about forty feet up in the air. School Meeting shut that one down too.

A couple more years later, we put it here in Alexander's scratchy spot."

Maia, another colleague, spoke next: "I didn't know about all that, but I've been on this swing in the current spot, and I don't think it's as dangerous as Leo does. It's fun."

Leo again: "I think we should take this one down, but we'll find another spot. No problem." We do have acres of woods.

After everyone who wanted to speak did so, we voted. Only two or three School Meeting members voted to keep the swing in its latest location. Leo reassured these that he would find a new branch to hang a swing. That afternoon, I saw him coming up the hill from the old swing site, a freshly cut rope in his hand. The boss, School Meeting, had spoken.

At another School Meeting, packed with students and staff members, several years earlier, Stephen, a teenager with some influence, had the floor and was pacing. "Look, I know this is difficult, but when are we going to get real around here?" he said. We were over an hour into a debate to expel a younger teenager. The JC had referred him to the JC Business section of School Meeting for sentencing after finding him guilty of another dangerous activity charge, this one involving matches. To open the debate, the JC Clerks had reviewed his long, serious judicial record. "What does somebody have to do around here to get kicked out?" Stephen asked, gesturing with his arms, rotating to face both sides of the spacious room.

School Meeting may be the ultimate act of faith in the student body at Fairhaven. No matter how egregious a student's behavior, two-thirds of the meeting must vote in order to suspend or expel him. Some students and all of the staff had spent the previous hour arguing for this expulsion to no avail. A silent coalition of computer gamers and combat boot-wearing punk rockers had voted against the motion. Stephen, a young man who skateboarded and who was also one of the school's experts in parliamentary procedures, had made a motion to reconsider the decision when the meeting could not agree to any subsequent motions.

"At this point, it's not even about him. It's about the school. There have to be limits," he argued. "Everybody knows about playing with matches. Like the staff said, these are both wooden buildings." How do you know when the tide turns? Sometimes the mood in School Meeting shifts; you can see it in people's eyes, maybe in the way they move in their seats. Stephen was getting through. "Nobody *wants* to kick anybody out, but sometimes we have to. I'm graduating from here next year, and I want my diploma to mean something. Vote to reconsider." He sat down.

We did, and later we voted to remove the student. School cultures have watershed moments. At Fairhaven, these often transpire at School Meeting, where we decide everything by vote, where each young person has the same power to vote and speak as each adult. Most moments at School Meeting are quieter, duller than expulsions. School Meeting approves visitors, purchase orders, and all changes to the Law Book.

Ernie Marconi raised his hand one day during Open Agenda, the section at the end of School Meeting when we entertain motions from the floor. "Okay, people, I've got an idea that's a little out of the box. Work with me," he began. At Fairhaven? We're the poster children for outside the box.

"I'm having this problem with my boss," he continued. "I was thinking there's a lot of wisdom in this room right here. Is there a way to tap into all your heads and solve this problem? I know it's probably not in order." He looked at me when he said the last bit, a nice move since I was about to raise my objection.

Somebody suggested a motion to informally discuss Ernie's

job. It was a stretch, but we had finished the agenda earlier than usual, and people wanted to work with Ernie. Nobody's fool, he had softened us up by naming our wisdom!

So we discussed his harsh boss at the pizza restaurant where he worked. People offered advice about workplace politics and communication options. Teenagers commiserated with stories of their own bosses from hell. I gave a pitch for not burning any bridges by giving two weeks' notice if he decided to quit. Hearing the variety of perspectives seemed to help Ernie. After the discussion, we adjourned.

A month later, and Ernie was soon to graduate. Various people had told him how they admired his creative use of School Meeting. Wanting to both memorialize himself and give others the chance to tap into School Meeting as a think tank for problems outside of Fairhaven itself, he moved to establish a "Marconi Section" on the agenda every week. Used here and there, but not every week, it remains on the agenda today.

I have my days around here, days punctuated by moments when I want to act unilaterally, to bypass School Meeting authority and process altogether. Teenagers have discovered Silly String. Maybe she's left her lunch out for the tenth day in a row. We need a new copier, and we need it now! How easy it would be to close the door to the office and decide how to deal with it alone.

Then I walk into the Chesapeake Room at one o'clock on Wednesday. Someone has just rung the big, old fashioned bell atop our pointed roof. Twenty or so students and all my colleagues sit in rows facing the Chair and Secretary. Their eyes are bright with purpose as they peruse the agenda. I note a ragged string of pre-teen boys in the back row and see the third item under New Business—"Move: Approve the new Computer Corporation procedures and re-open the computers." The Chair speaks, "I call the School Meeting to order." The boys join the rest of us in attentive silence as we begin the latest installment in the ten-year project of running the school. "Can the Secretary read the minutes from last week?"

Access to Power

Six-year-old June sat patiently throughout the long School Meet-ing, waiting for her agenda item, surrounded by the friends she had brought to support her motion. She leaned into my ear with a ques-tion.

"Where are we on the agenda?" Her loud whisper tickled.

"We're right here," I replied, pointing. "Yours is next."

We wrapped up the previous motion by voting, then the Chair, a teenage boy named Ryan, read June's motion aloud: "To let people run in the Chesapeake Room on Fridays. Is there a second?" Three of June's cohorts all said "Second," at the same time.

June spoke first: "Well, it's just that the Chesapeake Room is one of those rooms where it's really hard not to run, so we thought one day a week we should be able to. We like to run and practice gymnastics."

She was right. The room in question is very large, with a cathedral ceiling and huge windows looking out onto the forest. In addition to hosting meetings like this one, it's fabulous for Theater Corporation productions, dancing, and free play. Its maple floors invite running. Unfortunately, the Lawbook prohibits running indoors, and running across the Chesapeake Room disrupts people downstairs.

I wrote some bullet points for my turn to speak on the back of the agenda. I remembered bursting through the heavy doors at Little Flower at June's age for recess, the half-hour frenzy across the asphalt before Sister Agnes Mary rang the bell. Ryan called on me.

"I can remember what it feels like to want to run, run, run. Look at this room!" I checked my notes. "As School Meeting members may know, I've been advocating for quiet space in the building for years. Although I appreciate June coming to School Meeting rather than just breaking the 'no running' rule, I'm concerned because the JC Room is

right underneath the Chesapeake Room."

People agreed, and a colleague amended the motion by adding the phrase "except when JC is in session." After further discussion, we voted unanimously to approve running on Fridays. June and her buddies left, pumping fists and saying "yes" with gusto.

The Friday running rule stands, balancing the temptation to run the other four days of the week. With JC long since moved to the old building, people can run all day Friday. And thanks to June, run they do.

A Private Boat for Max:
Artistic Expression at Fairhaven

*...and an ocean tumbled by with a private boat for Max
and he sailed off through night and day and in and out of
weeks and almost over a year to where the wild things are.*

—Maurice Sendak, *Where the Wild Things Are*

ALMOST OVER A YEAR before he sailed off to graduation, a
Fairhaven student with extensive theater experience decided to
adapt Sendak's most famous book for the stage. His comprehensive creative process included studying the book, writing
and revising his script, making concept drawings and costumes,
and casting and directing the production. Audiences packed the
Chesapeake Room to witness the high-wire act of expanding
such a familiar children's book into a full-length play. With the

active support of the Theater Corporation, *Wild Things* became Matthew's private boat, an exclamation mark on his lengthy Fairhaven career, and a splendid example of how free students express themselves in the arts at Fairhaven School.

Every student seems to possess innate artistic tendencies and abilities. Like the boy who directed *Wild Things*, some arrive at Fairhaven with clear patterns of creative expression and expand upon them. Others find their way on campus. Some specialize, and some dabble in various modes. All seem to use some of their time to create things of beauty and meaning.

Art

From the beginning, the school attracted artists, both as founders and staff members. When we designed the first building, including an art room was an operating assumption, a no-brainer like having an office or bathrooms. From the first day, students have validated the assumption by spending time working in the art room and by voting to hire and re-hire artists.

The Art Room has always had a potter's wheel in one corner. For many years School Meeting hired a staff member who was a sculptor. When she left, a student took over clay work at school by providing instruction, pounding the clay, and cleaning the wheel. The potter's wheel has also been used for mastery of the unexpectedly difficult process of spin art. A number of orange trays bear name cards and ongoing plasticine projects, some of which are tiny, elaborately detailed rooms or towns, some of which are mere amorphous shapes used in elaborate two-person fantasy games.

A common sight in the art room is a crowd of people of different ages drawing at a table. What they draw fluctuates— abstract or realistic, animé, or pseudo-Disney, maybe holiday or get-well-soon cards for family or friends. The styles, content, and media change, but the behavior pattern remains. Whether using watercolors or markers, students influence one another's work, comparing and commenting as they go. Although sometimes they work in silence, they usually converse as they draw. The art room tables can be a vital think tank for discerning life's aesthetic joys and mysteries. One beaming little girl said as she took her paintings home, "Sometimes I think I'm the best artist in the world!"

Many times one of our staff artists will work on his own drawing while students work on theirs. Students will occasionally arrange a drawing class. Staff members also participate in the Art Corporation, the body that manages the room and ensures a steady flow of supplies. Another staff artist arranges informal and formal displays of student art and photography throughout the school. And those free-flowing table conversations? Staff members add their color to these as well, each according to his or her own style and inclination.

Last year the Gala Committee solicited help from the school's artists when decorating the Chesapeake Room for our annual tuition assistance fundraiser. To transform the room for the evening event, the Art Corp. bought many large, white paper lanterns and students began a week or two of intense, collaborative decorating. Many lanterns had flower patterns. Some were painted with more abstract designs. One was a charming geisha girl; another sported elaborate beetles. In addition to raising funds for the silent auction, the finished lanterns lighted the partygoers.

It's another day. An ear-splitting rattle jolts everybody in the old building. Those curious enough come to the shop that adjoins the art room discover the school's building manager/artist cutting metal with Diana. The shop always attracts both project participants and onlookers. These two spend the next month designing and building a very funky metal go-cart with salvaged materials, including old furniture wheels. Ever one to shock, Diana paints hers red, names it The Blood Bath. As often happens with art projects, another student designs a similar craft, painting hers yellow and naming it The Cheesemobile. Both undergo maiden voyages down the driveway, but most of their travel is imaginative.

With advances in technology, more and more students are taking pictures. For a few, photography has become a serious pursuit. Each student's unique vision develops over time through their photos—a foundling kitten, the ice-covered fairy tree, people wearing funny hats on the porch. Even our younger students have captured breathtaking images.

Aesthetic enthusiasms wax and wane in part with the skill sets of certain students or staff. One staff member had a second career as a hair stylist, and the open art room door would often reveal a student draped with a salon cape. Perhaps the staff member was demonstrating haircutting; perhaps Andrea wielded the scissors, learning to cut under his tutelage. As with shop projects, there was always a gaggle of students watching and commenting. Conversations flowed from haircutting technique to life's vicissitudes and back. Several years at school have been punctuated by psychedelic outbreaks of hair-dyeing-blues, pinks, purples, and greens. One or two JC cases have investigated claims of dye residue messes.

We've seen vigorously spiked hair and wild asymmetrical cuts. Students have grown hair well below their waists; some have arrived with severe buzz cuts or, in one memorable case, bald. Students have cross-dressed and experimented with makeup. Many fashions have graced the campus—renaissance-era bodices and hair nets, traditional prom gowns, high end, head-to-toe coordinated hip-hop outfits, straight suburban garb, and punk rock getups. If indeed a Fairhaven education represents self-knowledge, then all this energy and experimentation with one's appearance fits. Our campus and our ethos welcome the artistic pursuit of self-decoration as readily as it accepts the more generic appearances. Students feel safe to try on different looks, all on the path to deeper knowledge of self and how one fits into the community at school and into the larger community beyond our twelve acres.

Writing

Creative writing is a much more private mode of artistic endeavor on campus. Many students scribble in journals and blogs daily. One day in between JC cases I asked the clerk, a youngish teenager, what she wrote in her omnipresent journal. "Mostly inappropriate stories, you know, lots of violence and bad behavior," she replied. Her friend chuckled and confirmed the genre. I encouraged her to keep on writing.

A poetry workshop sprouted up in our ninth year, punctuated by two poetry nights where community members and invited poets read their work. As they progressed, student workshop participants stepped beyond the creative spark into the crucial tedium of revision. The young writers had spent considerable time rewriting each of their poems, and they read them as finished products. In contrast, for the second reading night, some younger students composed poems frantically minutes before the event, reading them with confidence as the ink dried. As with all the other arts modalities at Fairhaven, each writer found her own level. Unforced excellence emerges naturally, water flowing from a well.

Because graduates must write and defend a thesis, every year students are very motivated to improve their expository writing skills. Some prefer formal grammar and composition classes; others use their assigned thesis subcommittees to workshop their theses. Where does expository writing end and creative writing begin? Each informs the other. Poets who refine their skills by focusing on elements like diction and structure become better essayists, while a thesis writer looking for the right words to convey the importance of being JC Clerk may discover a poetic style. Writing is writing, and freedom allows Fairhaven's students to discover and foster individual voices, genres, and abilities.

Dance

Speaking of various genres, students have been dancing at school since we first threw open the oak doors in September, 1998. Nobody who was present will forget Sharon, Susie, and Jane choreographing then endlessly rehearsing their "I Want Candy" number for the talent show. Many years later, Susie was preparing to audition for performing arts schools. She passed a purchase order through School Meeting to hire an instructor for intensive training. For ten weeks she and a few other advanced students stretched and danced across the Chesapeake Room floor. In fiscal fairness, the School Meeting required the same instructor to offer an introductory class to beginners.

Dance and freedom seem to be a natural fit. Perhaps this explains the breadth of dancing styles crossing school floors during the first decade. Early on we hired a young man to teach Appalachian clogging. Talent shows have featured Irish step dancers, modern American dancers, and West African dancers. We have hosted contra dance fundraisers. One spring a staff member ignited the school with her passion for flamenco. Last year a parent donated salsa instruction. Hip-hop is happening. Still, perhaps the most intense grooving I've seen at Fairhaven was completely spontaneous. At the Music Corp's annual Valentine's dance, the deejays played some old school Parliament funk. Two young boys boogied until they sweated and nearly dropped, creating entire suites of unique dance moves in response to the other-worldly bass lines and towering horns. Totally Fairhaven.

Music
Students and staff have also been making music at school since the beginning. Again, given freedom to express and pursue interest, musicians thrive at Sudbury schools. Bass players and fiddlers, drummers and sax players have all filled the air with notes. Dozens have strummed guitars. Our pianos have earned their biennial tuning. From "Chopsticks" and "Heart and Soul" through the Dutch exchange student singing pop songs to the serious students of music theory, Fairhaven's keyboards get a workout.

Informal and formal mentorships often characterize Fairhaven musical careers. A parent who's a professional jazz musician led a four-piece band through a show-stopping set one year. Piano instruction is commonplace. One staff member has led African drumming groups on campus for two years. Some students prefer collaboration with one another, creating punk, rock and roll, and pop groups over the years. No mere cover bands, they've written songs together, typified by the sweet composition Patrice and Annette wrote and sang in honor of Andrea's graduation.

Another recent musical development on campus has been the mixing and creation on computers. Two students made and sold a CD of their music, and we anticipate more with the advent of the Digital Arts Corporation ("DA"). Led by two students and supported by a staff member and two volunteers with professional experience, the DA crowd carved out a room for computer-generated animation, sound mixing, and movie making and editing. Last year the corporation came of age when the campus was overrun by zombies—half the student body had plunged into an all-day short movie project. As digital arts expand, Fairhaven's students will explore new media with the same zeal and ability they've shown in older media.

Drama

Perhaps no corporation has blossomed at school quite like the Theater Corp. From a ragtag Christmas production of *St. George and the Dragon* in the unfinished new building to this year's *Peter Pan*, the Theater Corp. has grown into a money-making, viable force producing one or two shows per year. Like Matthew, the student who tackled *Wild Things*, one year another student wrote, designed, directed and starred in a *Batman* prequel he named *The Rise of the Dark Knight*. The Theater Corp. has put on everything from musicals to Shakespeare.

One year we voted to stage *West Side Story*. In a school of seventy students, would we find the singers, actors, and dancers to pull it off? Dynamic teens enlisted their friends, many of them first-time actors. Martial artists choreographed fight scenes; dancers spiced up the "America" number. A parent with vocal training coached both the Sharks and the Jets. A busy crew built a rooftop for Maria's song. By opening night, the old building and the new building seemed to adopt the play's rivalry. The run was a smashing success. Each performance was preceded by a spoof called *West Side Fried Chicken* written by a teen and acted by the littlest children.

Unlike other schools, participating in a play is not extra-curricular. A production begins as an idea that's pitched to the weekly Theater Corporation meeting. If there's a director and we like the concept, we vote to produce the play. Each play has to have a balanced budget before production. All of the elements of the play are responsibilities shared by staff and students via the corporation—writing/editing, set design and building, casting and directing, lighting and sound, even stage and house management. Many School Meeting members participate in each show, and each can polish her talent or explore new ones. Actors may paint backdrops; dancers might direct.

Each play to date has been a multi-modal testament to the arts at Fairhaven, a place where students sculpt artistic personae from the day they arrive. Like Sendak's Max, they don costumes and dance, they create worlds and they sing songs. They create what's real. They pretend. Whatever their experience, when they return from the faraway land that is Fairhaven, their rooms await them but they are forever changed, able to respond to their unique lives by creating things of beauty and significance.

Backstage at Midsummer

"Okay. Everybody quiet down." Fifteen-year-old Matthew stood on a chair in the very crowded kitchen. Only one bulb lit the cast. We had blocked the windows with newspaper to create privacy from eager theater-goers on the porch. It was opening night.

"I just want to thank you all for working so hard on this play. I'm honored to be directing you. When we first decided to do A Midsummer Night's Dream, *I had my doubts." Also in the cast as Oberon, he wore stage makeup and no shirt. "But you guys all learned your lines, and worked your butts off. We're ready."*

The costumed actors surrounding him ranged from novice to veteran, from age six to sixty. Robert, who would later bring down the house as Thisbe in drag, stood six and a half feet tall; Molly as little Peaseblossom was closer to four feet.

"People have been doing this play for four hundred years," I added. I had been voted in as assistant director. "Let's go make history."

In elementary school, my school plays were command performances—we all had to participate. I remember being one of many extras in Oliver! *I was at once jealous and terrified by my buddy Nick Dooley's singing lead role. Following* Midsummer's *brief run, I asked some Fairhaven actors if they had been scared, but I already knew the answer from their confident performances.*

"I just have one more thing," said Matthew. The crowd noise crackled through the low-tech speaker we'd set up to monitor from the kitchen. Actors shuffled in place, tugged at costumes. "One of my best teachers said what you should do on stage is tell a story. So, guys, go tell a story."

Down came the house lights. The actors for Scene One took their places. Small butterflies bounced inside me as I opened the script to follow the action, unable to join the silent card game some of the actors were dealing out.

Bridging Freedom and Liability

As soon as I saw the stream, I knew we had found our site.
From the beginning it has been the heart of Fairhaven School.

—Romey Pittman

WHEN I TOUR PEOPLE across the campus, we always end at the top of the steps overlooking the stream. Named Mt. Nebo Branch after an historic African-American church upstream, this evocative body of water borders our property. For many, the stream embodies Fairhaven. Its beauty intoxicates the visitors, flowing as it does beneath mature forest, across fossil deposits. The presence of a natural water feature on campus also raises questions and concerns in prospective parents, and therein springs a tale.

When the school founders were building the first building, they collected tons of deconstructed materials, including two steel, commercial-grade parking lot lampposts that were never used.[3] Imagine my surprise years later when I saw Robert and Saul dragging one out of its storage place beneath the solar panel enclosure. As they hefted the heavy pole across the playing field towards the woods, I had to ask what in the world they were doing. "We're building a bridge," one grunted in response.

Students had been mucking about in the shallow stream since before we opened the school—hunting for fossils, chasing frogs, playing pirates. While wading has been very common, crossing the stream is often part of the activity, and students have attempted many bridges. But a bridge with steel beams? This mission bore following.

The bridge project took place by the western edge of campus, near a piece of our property earlier students had mysteriously nicknamed "Choco Taco" after a popular, silly frozen confection. The generally shallow stream deepens there, forming a horseshoe around the land on the opposite side of the stream, giving it the feeling of a secluded peninsula. The bridge builders wanted reliable, dry-footed access to this haven, and many boys engaged in the multi-week venture of engineering and constructing. Girded firmly by the steel poles, the plywood bridge proved to be quite a reliable crossing. The satisfied crew members began claiming Choco Taco as their own land, moving abandoned furniture over the bridge and hanging a scary, "Keep Away" mask from a tree.

I was not the only School Meeting member who noticed their activity, however. Students of all ages and staff members had seen the flurry of building. We had all watched their treks across the field and down the shady, descending path that winds around thick beech trees before arriving at the big bend

in the stream. When they finished the bridge, we all started using it, creating two distinct problems for the builders. First, they
considered the bridge their property. They had designed it, collected its materials, and made it. They did not want to share its
use. Second, a steady flow of users negated the isolation Choco
Taco previously offered. They had built it, and we did come.

Tensions arose. The bridge builders guarded what they
considered their property with harsh words; younger members shoved visitors. Those who were shoved brought their
grievances to JC. The Committee charged the defendants with
harassment, but the tensions remained. Whose bridge was it?
The JC referred the issue to School Meeting. Borrowing from
Sudbury Valley's structure, I suggested to the bridge boys that
they incorporate.

Amidst the groaning that usually accompanies a restriction
on freedom, they met with me as their consultant on forming a
corporation to protect their property prior to School Meeting.
We covered basic corporate structure, then we brainstormed
their particular *raison d'être*—constructing and maintaining a
bridge. Could it be a private bridge? According to the Lawbook's
definitions of corporations, all corporations had to make their
activity or property available to all School Meeting members,
within reason. With most corporations, this has come to mean
users must become certified to use anything that is expensive or
dangerous, for example, the Kitchen Corporation's stoves and
knives, or attend a minimal number of corporation meetings
prior to gaining access to equipment or decisions.

But a bridge? We floated different ideas, but none satisfied.
Sometimes we at Fairhaven look to the larger community for
instruction, and the idea fell onto the table like two quarters
into a turnpike basket. Why not charge a toll of fifty cents for
non-corporation members who wish to use the bridge? Monies

collected could fund bridge repair and any future bridges. The corporation liked the idea and sent it, along with their proposed corporate charter, to School Meeting for ratification, which debated the question for some time. Proponents were impressed by the originality of the idea and by the prospect of relieving tensions at the stream. They also saw the bridge as belonging, at least in part, to its creators, so rewarding their corporation made sense. On the other hand, opponents sounded very much like people have sounded since ancient times when obliged to pay before road and bridge owners "turned the pike" aside to let them pass. They found the practice outrageous, expensive, and undemocratic. One of them found the proposal especially alarming: "Somebody said the bridge has a troll?"

Most School Meeting members, myself included, could see both sides of the toll issue. Here sat these young men who had concretized their first big project at school. They were willing to retrofit their activity to conform to the school's structure. Access to a more secluded area of the campus had always motivated them, and the toll protected this intention. At the same time, they had not incorporated early in the process, nor had they obtained permission to use the materials they had salvaged. Their manner with other School Meeting members, at times, had been much like the troll with the billy goats. By a narrow margin, we voted to grant the Corporation the right to charge tolls. In retrospect, perhaps the most lasting benefits of the project came from those meetings in which some bridge builders engaged in their first substantive, formal debates.

Very few people paid tolls, preferring to wade across. The school year was nearing its end, and neither the bridge nor Choco Taco itself were that great. People moved on to other things, including, eventually, the bridge builders themselves. Over the summer, a downpour washed out most of the structure, creating a headache for the Grounds Clerk, who brought the issue back to JC the following September as a mess. JC charged those bridge boys who had not graduated with leaving the mess, requiring them to clean it. New students have tried to replicate the bridge in the seasons since, but none have succeeded.

So the bridge story would remain a footnote were it not for another result. As progress often does, the bridge exposed a comparatively pristine part of campus to us all, including the deepest hole in the stream's entire length. One day a sweet, six-year-old visitor was playing on its banks, attracted to all the activity. His mother and a staff member chatted nearby. Imagine their surprise when the boy fell into the deeper water and went completely under. His mother yanked him out, scared but unchanged. Not so our stream policy!

Before that day, everybody had been free to go to the stream as they wished, regardless of age or experience. Our policy had been to post a sign that read "No Lifeguard on Duty. Use At Your Own Risk." Again, for almost all of its length, our stream's depth does not exceed the shins of our youngest students. After a big rain, the Grounds Clerk closes the stream until the water subsides. Prior to the episode at Choco Taco—the one spot deep enough to be over a small child's head—no incidents or concerns had compromised the freedom of students to ply the stream however they wished. When word of the mishap buzzed through campus, the Official Authorities Clerk and the Grounds Clerk agreed to close the entire stream to student activity until we consulted with both the school's attorney and the school's insurance agent.

Perhaps no advice from Sudbury Valley's founders has been as useful as their admonition to Fairhaven's founders to seek and retain good legal representation. Our attorneys have reviewed all of our corporate documents, especially those regarding our church school status. My questions never cease to amuse or bewilder them: Can students play paintball on campus? How about building a skateboard half-pipe? I've sent them dozens of other queries, from labor law questions concerning our unusual hiring process to copyright issues for the Theater Corporation. Looking back over the relationship, most of the school's questions have concerned liability, and the stream incident identified exposure that both the professionals and the School Meeting agreed had to be limited.

Closing the stream sent conversations raging through the school community like the stream itself after a thunderstorm. Some old-timers insisted that the boy falling in was a one-time event and that freedom to access the stream defined Fairhaven; any compromise would be unacceptable. Others demanded huge restrictions in access, concerned that now that we knew about the deep hole, we were even more liable. Most people agreed that we had to restrict the ability of our youngest students (we start with five-year-olds) to go to the stream alone, but were unclear about the rest.

We spent about a month fashioning our new policy. I filled half a yellow pad with legal advice. Not surprisingly, counsel advised us to allow no unsupervised students in the stream; School Meeting would have none of that. Over the course of one week, an idea to mark the deep spots with poles identifying height gained traction, then stalled. We finally voted to adopt a three-tier policy. Our youngest students could not go to the stream unsupervised by staff members. Those students in the middle age group could go to the stream with at least one other student, provided their parents had signed a waiver authorizing this. The oldest teenagers had complete access as before. Nobody has ever been allowed to swim on campus.

Back in the old days, as long-term students say, Fairhaven

School had fewer restrictions. One or two staff members drove students up the driveway on top of their cars. The rope swing found a stomach-turning temporary home, slung from a high branch over one of our steepest hills. Cyclists and skateboarders bombed down the paved driveway without helmets. As we have grown, so has our awareness and concern for the "L" word—liability. In each of these examples, the School Meeting has voted to limit freedom because of liability: riding on top of cars was forbidden, the rope swing had to be relocated, and riders of wheeled objects had to wear helmets.

No one restricts freedom lightly on campus. It defines us. Of course, School Meeting decision makers include the people whose freedoms are at stake. These debates have been as passionate as any at school, covering both legal advice and sentiment about the old days. We consider the importance of students taking risks, how essential it can be to their growth and development. We often align with community norms when the activity involves physical safety (for example the helmet rule). Once I invited our insurance agent to visit us and answer students' questions about requiring permission slips whenever a student rides in a staff member's car.

"No other school allows its teachers (sic) to drive students to get lunch every day," he began.

"But no other schools allow its students to choose how they spend their time every day. If we used the 'no other schools' rule of thumb, this place would be completely different," one student replied.

"The school is explicit in interviews about its program and its educational philosophy. And not having a curriculum does not risk the lives of its students. When we're talking about driving students, we're talking life and death," the insurance agent responded. Some heads nodded in the crowded room.

"Doesn't the school pay thousand of dollars a year for liability insurance? Why do we even pay it?" another student asked. A fair question.

"Yes, you do. But that insurance only covers teachers who are doing their jobs in a reasonable manner. If there were to be a tragedy, both the insurance adjustors in a claim and the judge or jury in a lawsuit would assess the reasonableness of the school's policies and actions. Signed permission slips are the standard for teachers driving students. In the case of teachers spontaneously driving students to get lunch, it doesn't pass the reasonableness test. It is not a necessary function of the job. It's not worth the risk, guys," he finished.

Checkmate. The tide turned just as it did with the stream policy, just as it has whenever the debate considers the value of a particular freedom versus the school's ongoing existence.

In a society that sees testing as innovation, and where lawsuits drop like leaves in autumn, Fairhaven School is precious to its staff and students, to its parents and founders. It feels, sometimes, like the small, life-saving blaze in Jack London's short story, "To Build a Fire." One little mistake in judgement— like building your life-saving fire under snowy branches or like a bridge leading to a serious injury—could douse it. When it comes to student safety and school liability, School Meeting remains vigilant to ensure Fairhaven's continued growth, adding one stick at a time to the fire, always watching for shifts in the wind.

Comparative Religion

What's The Deal With Ash Wednesday

Sitting in the enormous, Byzantine sanctuary of the Basilica of the National Shrine of the Immaculate Conception in Washington, DC, I had time to think. What had brought me here, twenty years after beginning my career in education? Two Fairhaven students sat with me in the wooden pew; we were on a field trip. I had attended parochial schools for twelve years, then taught in different Catholic schools for eight. Under this elaborate dome, my former schools echoed.

"What's the deal with Ash Wednesday?" Matthew had asked me, bounding into the office the day before. He was a teenager who'd attended Fairhaven for years.

Matthew knew my history, but it had been quite a while since I'd participated in the penitential rite. "Let's google it," I said. We did, and what I had learned as a grade-schooler at Little Flower came flooding back. Ash Wednesday marks the first day of Lent, the season preceding Easter in the church calendar.

"It's not one of the seven sacraments, but it is sacramental," I said to Matthew, a Reform Jew. Reading the computer screen, he looked confused.

"Ash Wednesday is a day of fasting and repentance. People use it to consider their transgressions, their sins. Catholics wear the ashes to symbolize cleaning their spirits before Lent," I offered. He still looked bewildered.

"Do you want to go check it out tomorrow?" I asked him.

No confusion this time. "Yeah, definitely. If you think it's okay." I knew he'd be respectful. We looked up schedules at the Basilica. Hey, I figured, let's go for the big show instead of the local parish. Another student jumped at the opportunity. They brought home permission slips, and the next day we drove the forty-five minutes into DC.

Along the way I gave them a crash course in Roman Catholicism, focusing especially on the sacraments and rituals. They asked a few questions, but it was mostly straight lecture. They were transfixed.

So there we sat. We breathed in the incense; we listened to the dolorous prayers, to the hymns of praise. Mid-day light poured through a rose-stained glass window onto the main altar, where the priest thumbed ashen crosses on the foreheads of the faithful. When I approached the sanctuary to receive my ashes, I invited Matthew to join me, just to come closer. He declined.

Afterwards, we toured the ornate building. Perhaps twenty smaller altars, most devoted to Mary, line the walls of the main church, differing wildly in styles and décor. We took in the green marble arch of Mary Queen of Ireland, the dour painted face of Our Lady of Czestochowa, and the bronze statue of Our Lady of Fatima in the golden narthex. We visited the Crypt Church, home to many more individual altars and the tomb of Bishop Shahan, the prelate who had championed the Shrine a century earlier. A mosaic of believers and pilgrims surrounded us at every turn.

The conversation in the car riding home touched upon the money needed to build the opulent basilica, the Church's teachings on social justice, and how Matthew's congregation views such matters. We compared our Irish grandparents. Had they supported Bishop Shahan's vision of a national shrine? Before pulling into the driveway at Fairhaven, we had cooked up a comparative religion course. By the time the class ended some months later, Matthew and six or seven others had heard presentations and asked questions of adherents from a variety of spiritual and philosophical traditions, including a Jew, a Muslim, a Yaqui Indian, a Wiccan, a Zen Buddhist, a Catholic, and an atheist.

Later that afternoon, the sun lengthened the shadows on the porch where Matthew and I sat. "Why is your forehead so dirty?" asked

Serge, a direct eight-year-old who was passing by.

"Show some respect," Matthew chided him. "It's Ash Wednesday."

Serge considered his transgression for a second, shrugged, then scurried down the porch. The bell pealed, signaling 4:50. Time to go home.

Persuasions

Kimberly and Stacy invited me to join them at the kitchen table. After some small talk—comparing lunches, trading samples, food restrictions—Alexander joined us. Knowing his likes, I offered him a corn chip. Kimberly asked "Hey, Alexander, do you want to join our club now that Francis isn't here?"

Talk of clubs at school always gets my attention. As Alexander considered the offer, I asked what kind of club they had. "Our dolls worship Spongebob and make him offerings of acorns," answered Stacy. Well, it had been a banner year for acorns on campus. She smiled at me, "It's just a game."

Alexander helped himself to another chip. Kimberly continued, "Well, Alexander, do you want to? Can you think for yourself?" A few years older than Alexander, Kimberly really wanted believers, maybe underlings.

His chip-scarfing over, Alexander responded as he walked away, "Praying to Spongebob is really boring."

I heard later from a JC Clerk that the girls had brought Francis, a fellow student from a devout family, to JC, where Stacy pressed their complaint: "We were playing this game where our dolls worship Spongebob and Francis said we would go to hell for it. It scared us, especially Alexander. We felt threatened."

The JC walked the tightrope before them, ending up charging Francis with the bedrock rule we adopted from Sudbury Valley's lawbook in our first year: "No one may knowingly or negligently infringe on anyone's right to exist peaceably." He pled guilty and JC gave him a warning.

A Survey

On the old building porch, a clump of teenage students and I discussed the existence of God, and what we believe. Our quick survey results:

> *two Christians*
> *one Wiccan*
> *two agnostics*
> *one atheist*
> *one lapsed Catholic*

We found more common ground than bones of contention, more respect than mockery. An acorn clanged onto the green metal roof. Perhaps the looming congregation of trees kept us civil.

Tolerance

Another day. JC had called in two older students. Jake, who had brought this complaint, spoke first: "I told Marla that I don't believe in God. I should have the right to say that. She started harassing me." The JC Clerks exchanged knowing looks. Here we go again.

Viola, one of the clerks, called on Marla. "We were talking and Jay said he doesn't believe in God over and over," she said. "I told him if he doesn't stop, I'll write him up. He didn't stop." A line of questioning ensued.

> *Did Jake make fun of Marla's beliefs?*
> *No.*
> *Did he express his disbelief in a mocking way?*
> *No.*
> *Did he follow her around, harassing her?*
> *No.*

The Clerks wrote their report. By vote, JC dropped the case. When she stood, Viola revealed her T-shirt, one that resembles a popular bumper sticker, spelling "COEXIST" with various religious symbols for the letters (Islamic moon for "C", Star of David for "X", yin/yang for "S", cross for "T", and so on.) A paragon of pluralism, she admonished Marla and Jay: "Everybody has a right to believe what they want to believe here, guys, okay?"

One of Life's Big Questions
Anecdote from Alexander's father, a month later:

"Daddy, Daddy, you won't believe what Sunshine thinks is true. She thinks that when you die you come back as somebody else! Do you think that when you're dead you stay dead, or do you come back as somebody else, maybe even a puppy?"

Each New Student a Universe

As I drove up the driveway to drop students off following a field trip, a dozen young people milled around a new, large wooden structure. Several were painting the two-by-fours purple. What is it today? *I wondered.*

Upon closer inspection, I learned that they had built a giant slingshot, with surgical hose for the launching mechanism. Their projectiles included tennis balls and wads of masking tape. James and Gary, two new teenagers, were primary architects of the project, nicknamed the "Pultacat" (a rearranging of catapult.)

Unsatisfied with the prototype, the next day they gave it to some younger students and began working on version two. Their crew spent the next week building a more successful device, then firing various objects (including sandwiches) across the field. Naturally, JC adjudicated a few cases involving allegations of Pultacat messes, disruption of activity, unauthorized use of Art Room paint, and dangerous activity. Nobody was hurt.

Each student who joins Fairhaven brings unique interests, personality, and sensibility to the evolving mix on campus. The vegan girl who grafittis her car. The drummer who plays in a metal band. The Shakespeare enthusiast who's an Irish step dancer. The poet, the nature girl, and the reader in the porch rafters.

James, the Pultacat builder, is a charismatic military strategist, and at Fairhaven he has found plenty of people to share this interest. A week after the Pultacat, he and his friends pushed four tables together in the Chesapeake Room for a massive Warhammer campaign, with some two hundred tanks, soldiers, and weapons arrayed against each other. They've crafted a motion to charter the Ballistics Corporation at School Meeting to regulate and manage their launching equipment. As he makes his mark on the culture, James has taken under his calm, good natured wing a much younger, more mercurial student who had been running into difficulty in JC of late. A lieutenant, if you will.

Two Streams: Evidence of Life

Little Falls

Sister Mary Patrick stood just outside the double doors at recess, a large brass bell in one hand. In seventh grade we played football on the asphalt, tearing into one another with all the fervor of boys who had been sitting all day. I slammed into Jack Halloran after he caught the ball and next thing I knew we had crossed into a fight. Soon his knees pinned my arms until I gave up. A swim team star, he was stronger than he looked. By then the bell's urgent rings signaled the earnest approach of nuns to break up what was already over.

I tally the hours at Little Flower in my head, year after year after year. Specific memories punctuate the count—winning the spelling bee by making it through "galloping;" accidentally pegging poor Steve Harris in the face in murder ball, knocking off his glasses; feeling the brief liberty of walking to the office with a teacher's message

Bloodthirsty chants of Fight! Fight! Fight! *echoed in my ears as I crossed Little Falls Parkway onto the path through the woods that afternoon. I yanked off the green and black plaid uniform tie, stuffed it in my book bag. Is there a more solitary sound than a single crow calling?*

Stepping down the bank, I began following the creek rocks that led to my neighborhood. Raccoon tracks in the sand stopped me, tiny handprints spread beside a pile of purple-lined snail shells. I pocketed three empty shells. Where gray boulders accelerated the water, fingerling minnows idled in the eddies, as if waiting to shoot the rapids, to find the nerve, maybe, as the water fell over rocks. I wish I could say that I resolved that day to start a better school when I grew up, to make a different childhood possible. I wish I'd resolved to change my path, that I'd decided, like Milton, to fly this cursed place.

Are minnows baby fish or just small? Will they ever get the nerve? After watching this little school above the falls a few minutes, I made my way home, searching the remainder of the stream for evidence of life.

Mt. Nebo Creek

School Meeting had hired a friend and neighbor to replace the steps to Mt. Nebo Creek, Fairhaven's stream, with steps made of black locust blocks. We had decided on locust because the wood is so hardy and rot resistant. Descending the steep stairway, I remembered reading that gold-diggers in California used locust to support their mineshafts, even planting groves of eastern locust for future mines. Heading to the stream often feels like treasure hunting.

A line of students trailed me away from the hubbub of the two buildings down, down to what used to be the ocean floor. At the foot of the steps, those with shoes left them on the bank and we were in the water, cold enough to hurt the first few minutes. The streambed is stone hard, created by eons of compacted ocean diatoms, so it really is a floor.

Fifty paces from where we entered, the floor separates a foot or so, making a clean break that causes a waterfall. Like most days, we occupied the waterfall for a few minutes, an unspoken ceremony. Our feet reddened, used to the chill now. Bella poked the bank with a stick in search of fossils. A dragonfly flew by, causing a buzz among the students who saw it.

Co-founder Romey Pittman had scrambled me down the steep, stream-carved hill first, stairless at the time, to show me the property before we built the school. The first shark's tooth I found was whisper clean, sharp to the touch, with smaller points to each side of the main tooth. A keeper. Bella showed me her latest tooth—only one point, but larger than my first. We followed Charlie downstream.

"They think this part of the ocean was a whale calving area, and sharks attacked them here," I said, passing time as we sifted the fresh

gravel piled beyond the giant fallen log. We identified the fifteen mil-lion year-old shark species by shape—the wider teeth are makos, those with serrations are tigers, straight and thin fossil teeth like Bella's used to grow in sand sharks' mouths. We didn't find any great whites. Three students sat astride the log over us, their feet hanging free. Not treasure hunters themselves, they were lost in a game. Time slowed to the stream's pace.

A heavy rainfall had rushed the narrow part of the stream, no wider than the Circle Room in the old building, so the Grounds Clerk had posted the sign STREAM CLOSED the day before. Concern over liability circles the campus like the ancient sharks around the baby whales, so we close the stream when it's up. After the storm, Charlie knew fresh teeth awaited. Aside from the cold, the stream could not have been more harmless one day after the thunderstorm.

Charlie found a handful of teeth among the stones that day. At School Meeting the following Wednesday, he obtained permission to bring them home after a month in the Circle Room display case, just above the deer skull. He pestered me at least once a week, naming the teeth and where he found his favorites, until the day he finally brought his evidence of ancient life home to add to his collection.

Until I Lift the Earth
I Cannot Move

The buildings at Fairhaven are only
for warming up or cooling down.

—a Fairhaven student

A TEENAGE GIRL APPROACHES holding a small, shiny brown snake coiled around her finger. "Did you meet Betty?" Andrea asks. She tells me it's a worm snake that she found under a rotting log on campus. She'll keep it for a few days, arranging an intricate habitat of moss and leaves in an aquarium that becomes Betty's temporary home in the Art Room. Dozens of students will touch her and observe her before Andrea releases the snake later, careful to let it go where she had captured it. An inveterate taxonomist, I look up worm snakes in the *Reptiles and*

Amphibians field guide, sharing the entry with interested young people.

Writer Richard Louv, in his *Last Child in the Woods*, identifies a cultural shift away from the outdoors in the lives of American children. He names a host of reasons for the shift, including suburban and urban planning, families where both parents work, parental fears, increased scheduling, more homework from schools, and video and computer games. He has, indeed, codified a massive change in the American landscape, one he names "nature-deficit disorder." At risk, he postulates, are the spiritual, physical, and mental health of our young people.[4]

Fairhaven sits atop her hill in contrast to this prevailing deficit. For many Fairhaven students, being outside is their predominant educational choice. Weather permitting (and sometimes weather notwithstanding), a visitor will see students outdoors—at one of our picnic tables, playing basketball or four square, in the fields, in the forest, perhaps in the stream. They build tree houses and fairy houses. They collect creatures like Betty. They swing and they seesaw. The Munchkins train. They read on the porches and they play in the piles of leaves for as long as they like.

Fairhaven's campus comprises twelve acres of hardwood forest and fields. A shallow stream with a waterfall marks the property line on one end. As the seasons pass, flora and fauna come and go as well, enriching the student body and deepening the institutional fabric of the school.

June and Maureen came to the office one spring day to ask me to join them in the woods. We passed the swing set and ducked beneath oak branches to enter the forest, where hundred-foot tall tulip poplars create a canopy. As we descended, the gentle waterfall murmured. My small guide June said, "We found a trail. Do you want to come?" Who could resist?

Following the trail I noticed wildflowers on the forest floor—the spiral unfurling of May apples and the delicate pink and white blooms of spring beauties. Where the trail rises beside the stream, they advised caution while breaking into a skip. Soon they were chanting in syncopation: "May apples and spring beauties! May apples and spring beauties!" After climbing over a massive fallen beech tree and scrambling up a hill, we emerged at the other end of campus.

"Let's do it again!" they exclaim. The office could wait.

For many Fairhaven students, arriving at school means kicking off their shoes. Thus their feet literally touch the ground on campus. The rest of their bodies soon follow, and they contact the outdoors for countless hours. Theirs is an experiential way of learning about nature, studying it, if you will. Call it whole body science, where the people immerse themselves in the physical world. Perhaps they will make connections through someone else's knowledge as we did informally with the field guide. What they get now is the physical foundation.

Another day three different young girls approach with fists full of onion grass. "Want to try some?" asks one. Her breath reeks. I decline and they hurry away in search of more pungent shoots for the soup they made that afternoon. Six months later another constellation of students harvests paw paws, a native fruit also known as the poor man's banana. They delight in eating its yellow, custard-flavored pulp.

The foundation of an old homestead sits just inside the forest. Every spring a splash of yellow and white daffodils evoke an anonymous former resident's flower garden, and every year students discover these and collect them. Sometimes they bring them inside to decorate the school, sometimes they weave crowns and decorate themselves; and at least once they carried them throughout the school trying to sell them.

Our twelve-acre campus is home to scores of deciduous trees, including oaks, beeches and poplars. When the days shorten, autumn winds blow the multicolored leaves to the ground. Our students chase the falling leaves, making wishes on those they catch. A one-handed catch is most auspicious. This annual game typifies the school—outside, connected to natural cycles, spontaneous, unpredictable, and ephemeral.

The floor of the stream behind the daffodil site is part of a massive Miocene epoch fossil deposit that includes the noted Calvert cliffs site on the Chesapeake Bay. When students and I wade in the ankle deep water, we are traversing clay deposits that used to be the floor of a warm, shallow ocean some twenty million years ago. Fossils erode from the steep clay banks to appear in piles of gravel, and strong rains wash new treasures from upstream. Students have found a variety of shells and hundreds of sharks' teeth. School Meeting has established a display case for these discoveries in the old building.

At The Graveyard
Members of homeschooling families, Fairhaven's very first students had the freedom to explore a beach in the town of Fairhaven, some twenty miles southeast of the school's permanent home. Their most passionate pursuit in that first year was fossil hunting on the beach, with sharks' teeth their prime quarry.

"Let's go to the graveyard," Saul said upon arriving at the co-op one fall morning. A devoted fossil hound by then, he wanted to go there every day. He rolled his dice across the Parcheesi board as we waited for the other three bone collectors. After they arrived and checked in, we took the ten-minute walk down the beach to our favorite spot. It was so full of fossils, the students had nicknamed it the "graveyard."

November wind had blown red and gold leaves into the Chesapeake. I looked over at Saul, who was complaining about the leaves covering his piles of gravel. He was on all fours, his nose three inches from the ground as he scanned for fossilized treasure. He was in his rhythm now—his hands sifted the pebbles, then he searched each pile, crawling along the shore to the next spot when he finished. Occasional yelps meant he found a tooth, perhaps a bone. Three other boys and I were also hunting.

Two dozen geese cruised the blue overhead, their sharp calls steadier than Saul's. Soon the Bay would fill with wintering ducks, geese, swans, and even loons. Blue-winged teal had already passed through. Hearing the geese had set the boys to honking.

"You find anything yet, Saul?" asked Jamie with a competitive tone.

"Of course. About ten teeth so far, but I'm just getting warmed up."

"Anything as big as this?" Jamie had moved next to Saul, holding a fine two-inch mako in Saul's face.

Bragging just went with fossil hunting for these guys. I was searching under some big rocks. I reached for something dark and pulled up a chiseled, flat black stone with notches. It came to a point. "Arrowhead!"

They all gathered to admire my find. Native Americans had settled the Chesapeake thousands of years ago, and their tools washed up on shore from time to time. Our conversation turned to what their life may have been like, why they lived on the water, even Captain John Smith. After a few minutes, Saul couldn't stand it: "Gimme that arrowhead! I'll trade you all my teeth for it." Crossing the bridge that led back to the co-op, I reminded him that I didn't trade.

Wild Life

In our second year a handful of young students met and be-friended "Blue," a blue jay that had taken up residence where the backyard meets the woods by the seesaws. With patience and diligence, they earned Blue's trust. Okay, they also fed Blue. Soon the jay would perch on one student's finger. Every day they would visit with Blue, care for him. For a month or two they spent most of every day with a feral bird friend.

In contrast, another year a colleague arrived with a barred owl she'd just found dead in the road. Teenagers asked me if they could dissect it. First, I told them they had to call a Special School Meeting for permission to do so. In the two hours re-quired after posting notice of such a meeting, school members began the debate in conversations. Passions burned on both sides of the issue. Along with one of the interested students, I contacted a birding friend for advice about both the legality and the technique to dissect a raptor.

At School Meeting we discussed many aspects of the pro-posed activity. Students with animist or New Age beliefs ob-jected to the dissection out of respect for the owl's spirit. Safety-minded individuals ensured antiseptic procedures, amending the students' motion to include specific language about how and where the dissection must occur. One staff member with taxidermy experience extolled the value of boiling the carcass. Weighing these and other factors, School Meeting voted to ap-prove the dissection.

Several people watched and joined as they dissected the owl on a folding table in the backyard. Some hours later, they boiled the carcass to more easily expose the skeleton. The lead dissector took home the deep-eyed skull.

Every spring a buzz passes through the school: "the skinks are back!" So begins the annual process of spotting, chasing, and collecting some of the local population of five-lined skinks as the quick lizards warm themselves in the sunny areas near our buildings. Some students have caught skinks each year the school has been open. More than one has learned that the primary skink defense mechanism is a tail that detaches (only to regenerate later). One year it was my honor to spot the first skink, and my announcement induced a frenzy among students that resembled the wiggly lizards themselves, as intrepid Fairhaveners chased them to and fro.

In a recent year an even louder buzz sounded at Fairhaven when the largest seventeen-year cicada cycle, known in the scientific community as "Brood X," emerged on campus. Before long students were wearing live cicadas, showing one another cicada gender distinctions, and arguing for and against cicada rights in JC. On an overnight field trip to Catoctin Mountain State Forest, several students entertained insects on their very own man-made cicada amusement park complete with a roller coaster and carousel. Again, they had the time and interest to fully explore the unique phenomenon of millions of noisy, red-eyed insects appearing on campus for over a month, and they embraced the opportunity. Towards the brood's end, one student showed me her cicada graveyard. In the shade of a maple tree, she had established a plot with dozens of august markers arranged in precise rows.

Total access to the natural world means total access to weather. Students sled in the snow and sunbathe in the sun. More than once I've seen young people standing under an eave letting the runoff from a deluge soak them. There are always students who run outside in a heavy rainstorm and dance and sing in what can only be described as joy. Singin' in the Rain.

Sometimes, wild encounters at school border on the fantastic. One day I arrived and read a sign on the front door:

"WOODS CLOSED. COUGAR SIGHTING." Now Fairhaven's campus is bucolic, but we're not far from highways, fast food, and suburbia. I chuckled at the thought of North America's only big cat prowling our small woods. Sharon and Jane approached me and swore they'd seen a cougar from afar. They described its tawny color, the length of its tail, even the feline quality of its leap into the woods. They took me to the websites, showing me the cougar photographs, reading me the descriptions. "That's what we saw. I know it," Sharon said. Jane nodded, adamant.

We called Animal Control, and soon a helicopter was circling our property! The woods took on an air of foreboding as people scanned its edges for signs of the elusive predator. Theories raced through both buildings. An escaped exotic pet? A miraculous mountain cat that had come down from the Alleghenies hundreds of miles to the west? Sharon and Jane stuck to their story. My colleagues and I spent the day reassuring students and parents that our woods were safe. I also spoke with wildlife experts.

Eventually the Grounds Clerk reopened the woods. The cougar grew in stature with time, a genuine Fairhaven School legend. Our basketball team even adopted the cougar as its mascot.

A month later as I was closing the school, a neighbor approached and asked if I had seen his missing dog, a large brindle boxer. He saw a sign about our cougar and said with a smile that his lost pet could be mistaken for a cougar. To this day the students who spotted the animal deny this canine explanation. The legend lives.

Of course what is missing from these stories are adults seizing moments in nature to edify the children about taxonomy, the scientific method, or other abstractions. Driven by my own curiosity or our shared interest, I have looked up five-lined skinks and other critters in field guides with students, and I have checked the Internet with students for information about the transit of Venus or other natural phenomena. I definitely leafed through field guides and visited websites after the "cougar" encounter with students.

So why not do it whenever I see the chance? Seize the moment? In the culture of Fairhaven, my interactions with students must remain genuine, an outgrowth of our relationship and interests. Crucially, if I want to be rehired, I must recognize the subtle distinction between the sincere flow of information and one person educating the other. The free children at Fairhaven recognize the disrespect of adults who push information on them like water in a stream recognizes an impediment. Usually, the impediment is small and they can flow around it; sometimes it blocks the whole stream and they stagnate. Regardless, as soon as someone intervenes in an unnatural way (think, "Oh my, that's a five-lined skink! Do you know its Latin name?") the student's education about the natural world has ceased, and her ongoing education about relationships with well-meaning people who don't understand the nature of the school or the nature of learning has resumed.[5]

Nature writer Louv examines solutions to the troubling shift away from nature in the lives of twenty-first century children. His proposals include increasing attendance at summer camps, comprehensive plans for re-wilding our cities, and re-populating the prairies with homesteads and smaller, interconnected towns. Among the proposed ways to reconnect children with nature is a chapter entitled "Natural School Reform" wherein he cites examples of schools addressing the problem. Still, the author recognizes their limitations: "To suggest that ecoschools, schoolyard greening, and experiential education programs are representative of a major movement would be misleading, but the numbers are increasing."[6] His book is a serious treatment of the disturbing cultural trend of de-naturing children and the small but growing resistance to it. We plan to let him know about the holistic experiences of Fairhaven students and students at Sudbury schools worldwide.

Our schools offer an educational approach to the natural world that is unique both for its freedom and its breadth. Free to discover and explore on Fairhaven's twelve acres, our students connect with the natural world. They touch and taste this world, hear it and see it. They delight in its living components. They transform from distinct "others" to united elements of the biosphere and become, finally, a part of the landscape, scores of young people now sentient features of the particular piece of the world they inhabit.

Writers name this level of connection. First, Kentucky poet Wendell Berry:

> I am wholly willing to be here
> between the bright silent thousands of stars
> and the life of the grass pouring out of the ground.
> The hill has grown to me like a foot.
> Until I lift the earth I cannot move.[7]

And from Colorado, Pattiann Rogers names how a Fairhaven student may feel at the end of a day, as evening shadows darken the stream:

> All afternoon I part, I isolate, I untie,
> I undo, while all the while the oak
> shadows, easing forward, slowly ensnare me,
> and the calls of the wood peewees catch

and latch in my gestures, and the spicebush
swallowtails weave their attachments
into my attitude, and the damp sedge
fragrances hook and secure, and the swaying
Spanish mosses loop my coming sleep,
and I am marsh-shackled, forest-twined,
even as the new stars, showing now
through the night spaces of the sweet gum
and beech, squeeze into the dark
bone of my breast, take their perfectly
secured stitches up and down, pull
all of their thousand threads tight
and fasten, fasten.[8]

When the bell rings to mark the end of the day, satisfied members of the student body go home wet from the stream, covered in dirt, or clutching a new favorite stick. Fossils and feathers line their pockets—little pieces of their encounters with the land beneath their feet.

This Endless Calling

"Up here,
         see me"—*you guys hear that?*

I'm pointing to forest canopy,
where April treetops
                    gleam golden.
Two students listen, coaxed
from the porch rockers,
to hear the newly nesting
                    red-eyed vireo.

Two weeks later,
I've brought three this time,
to just inside the treeline.
         Trilling
                  toad calls
                           overlap,
casting us for a scene
in a fifties horror movie.
We all get a little spooked.

That's pretty cool says one.
Yeah, awesome, another.

And then we migrate
back to the schoolhouse,
silent but for

         last year's leaves.
I'm finished saying
what I know.

Above us,

         a sleeping owl
dreams the call he'll later
       whoop
from the stream-carved hollow,
   a call I savor alone,
this gift,

       this endless calling.

Failure is Part of Our School

Failure is instructive. The person who really thinks learns quite as much from his failures as from his successes.
—John Dewey

Whenever you fall, pick something up.
—Scientist Oswald Avery, on failure

A TEENAGER ROLLERBLADES on the metal rails that lead to the parking lot at school. He gains speed, then hops up and rides the curved surface to its end, sometimes adding tricks like a three-sixty to his ride. Following the skateboarders before him, his repetitive work colors Fairhaven's landscape, and offers daily opportunities to understand the school. One day I watched as he tried to negotiate the entire length of the rails, including two ninety-degree turns. Over and over, gravity and centrifugal force knocked him off. Over and over, he skated back up the sidewalk to try again. His experience demonstrated determination, commitment, and moxie. His actions also exemplified the value of failure, an aspect of learning and life that underlies so much of Fairhaven School's education.

Like the intrepid rollerblader, our students often choose activities they know will result in repeated failure. Novice actors step to the stage, rusty writers attempt five paragraph essays, and social neophytes navigate the teen milieu. Recall that all of these and countless others are chosen challenges. Why not just hang out? Why do we see young people from year to year who push themselves into steep learning curves?

People thrive when we trust them. With intrinsic motivation, time, and a supportive community, our students lurch into motion, humming along into a unique educational experience. Although one marvels at the lions and tigers in circuses as they jump through the trainer's hoops, imagine the leaps the big cats in the wild make without the hoops! Likewise, the challenges of each Fairhaven student's real life produce both close calls and awe-inspiring leaps.

Our judicial process handles mistakes and failings with little fanfare. Most students spend some time in JC addressing complaints with little or no parental notification. They learn from their errors. Each year a handful of students develop thick files of grievances, spending dozens of hours in the JC room accounting for their various deviations from community norms and laws. Feedback comes from peers, older and younger students, and adults. A successful JC reserves intense scrutiny on rule breaking for serious events, treating serial messes and annoyances more like parking tickets. Students who may spend a year or two breaking minor rules can take their "failure" in stride, since everyone else is, and learn from their mistakes.

Sometimes the mistakes can be pretty major. A furious first-year student punched another student in the computer room. The JC investigated the allegation and charged him with rules prohibiting harassment and dangerous activity. Because of the serious nature of the offense, the JC also voted to refer him to School Meeting for sentencing. After reading his prior offenses, community members debated sentences; more than a few connected his violence to the gaming environment. School Meeting suspended him for a week and restricted him from all video and computer gaming for three months after his suspension.

He carried out his sentence with distinction, reading novels and widening his social network at school. Following his ignominious, ruffian violent beginning, this young man became a rock-solid member of our school—School Meeting Chair, Law Clerk, evening custodial employee. Now he's a college student. When asked about his career at Fairhaven, he often begins the discussion by saying the colossal mistake he made and the resulting sentence became a turning point in his life. Sometimes he reminds whoever's listening that the written Chinese character for crisis is made up of both the character for danger and the character for opportunity.

A few students spend more than the usual amount of time stalled, or in crisis. Picture someone clinging to a cliff, scrambling to get up. On campus, they may not follow through on things, or their choice may not seem to prepare them for their next step into the world. We even embrace this more comprehensive type of failure, remembering that our premise still applies: you are in charge of your education. If the education you created at Fairhaven hasn't prepared you for what's next, that failure may be the one that teaches the most about life.

In the scientific community failure is called trial and error. An essential component in the scientific method is the failure of an hypothesis and the scientist's ability to learn from her mistake. All religious traditions and spiritual journeys accept and embrace human failings as those things that make us human. Only by failing can one approach the divine. Our mistakes presage our growth.

Yet prominent cultural institutions reject failure: the military, sports, and schools. It seems every war movie declares "failure is not an option." Of course we recognize that failure is anathema to military success. Likewise, in competitive sports, teams play to win, and winners gain trophies, accolades, professional contracts and endorsement deals. Losers are...losers. Legendary football coach Vince Lombardi put it this way: "Winning isn't everything, it's the only thing."

Still, military strategists and sports enthusiasts recognize and embrace failure's value. Again, Lombardi: "The greatest accomplishment is not in never falling, but in rising again after you fall." This describes our rollerblader's process. Churchill writes, "Success is going from failure to failure without a loss of enthusiasm."

Compulsory schools reject failure out of hand, assigning people who fail low grades. Perhaps mistakes will garner a low class rank, maybe even a separate, slower educational track altogether. Schools often drive out students who continue to fail. Many teachers and schools gin up the grades to mask the perception of failure. In mainstream education, failure is truly not an option. Nevertheless, so many students do fail, and instead of being able to learn from their mistakes, drop out or go on into adulthood convinced that they're stupid or hate math.

Students learn and study for the sake of the activity at Fairhaven. When explaining the school to visitors, we tell them about the freedom from compulsory curriculum. Sometimes the next question is, "Do you have grades and report cards?" When our younger students play school, yes, we do have grades. Otherwise, no. As a society, we have come to rely on external, sometimes arbitrary grades to identify success or failure. Fairhaven and the other Sudbury schools reject grades as a reasonable system. Labeling someone and his work a "D" or an "F" can damage a child's self-confidence and sense of self. Labeling someone and her work an "A" can create damage of a different kind-- a sense of entitlement, or dependency on praise, or anxiety.

Our approach challenges each student to develop her own agency, basing it on internal drives and real world externalities, rather than scales of letters, numbers and caprice. In the absence of arbitrary evaluation, students grow in their own time, for their own reasons. Failure becomes part of their lives, no more, no less. At Fairhaven we recognize that failure is often a necessary stage on the way to success, and welcome, or at least grit our teeth through the failures and fiascos. Then late one afternoon we see and celebrate when a sweaty, tired teenager jumps up on the rails one more time and rides them all the way down.

What the Coup Didn't Do

IN MAY OF 2000, George sauntered in to the weekly School Meeting, approaching the table where the Chair and Secretary sat. Two teens followed him, wry smiles crossing their faces. With exquisite timing, as if he had rehearsed it in his head, he dropped a set of documents on the table, declaring, "Here are your new rules!" With that, he turned on his combat-booted heel and left, again trailed by his comrades.

Those of us in School Meeting looked at each other. Some shrugged. The Chair scanned the document. "I think we may have a problem," he said.

We were finishing our second tumultuous year. We only had one building, so School Meeting took place in what we then called the Activity Room. Several staff members and a handful of students sat on folding chairs facing the School Meeting officers' table. "Well, what does it say?" I asked, not a little bit impatient.

"Apparently they've been holding a series of Special School Meetings for weeks now, during the regular School Meeting," said the Chair, leafing through the delivered papers.

"Let me see that," I said, approaching the table, all decorum lost.

"They can't do that!" said a colleague.

"We can, and we did." George and more of his crew had re-entered, unable to resist the reactions, the cats who had swallowed a whole flock of canaries. He continued. "You see, your Lawbook has a loophole, and we found it. Nowhere does it say that a special School Meeting cannot take place Thursdays at one o'clock." One of the cats giggled.

Your Lawbook. For over a year George had been watching School Meeting, both from the back of the room and from the Chair's seat. To be sure, we were still finding our legs as a democratic school. He had seen the preponderance of staff attendance and opinions, the growing indifference of his fellow teens. They had concluded that School Meeting was too staff-dominated, and they had acted.

Posting the required notification of a special School Meeting on a postage stamp-sized piece of paper on the designated bulletin board, then electing substitutes for the absent officers, again by the book, they had been running parallel meetings for a few weeks. George's documents were the meticulous minutes of their decisions kept by Wanda.

I rifled through the red-bindered Lawbook to check their actions against the letter of the law. "It looks like this may be legit, although it clearly flies in the face of the democratic principles of the school," I said, buying time.

"We may debate that later, Mark. But am I correct in your assessment as Law Clerk that these special School Meeting decisions stand?" I could have throttled him. Deep breaths, I thought. Deep breaths.

"I move we recess School Meeting until tomorrow at one, so I can review these," I said, holding the minutes high. The teens looked at George. Somewhere, a clock ticked a few slow seconds.

"I second the motion," he said. Everybody present voted to do so. Détente. They had ground School Meeting to a halt, and their glee was as palpable as my rage. I wish I could say I understood and appreciated their action at the time, but fury was all I felt as I went to a quiet room to read the minutes.

Special School Meeting
Topic: Rules

(*Motioned and Passed*):
George: Elected Chair
Wanda: Elected Secretary

School Meeting came to order at 1:15.
Motion: To repeal 2-32-01 (the rule requiring a second reading for rule changes). Passed.
Motion: To close this School meeting to all those not on initial list. Passed.

Already out of order. They closed their meeting to other students as well! And striking the second reading rule? Yikes.

Motion: The students shall be the only members of the School Meeting that may vote on, alter, or pass rules regarding student issues. The staff may only vote on, alter, or pass rules regarding staff issues. Staff issues are defined as any issues that fall under the following categories: closing school, extraordinary use of campus, committees, clerkships, office machines, staff sick days, staff attendance policies, emergency school closings. Student issues are defined as anything that is not included in the staff issue definition.

Substitution: No staff member shall make a motion affecting students without a student sponsor. Accepted into main motion.

Amendment: No staff member may make a motion affecting the content of the Lawbook without a student sponsor. Accepted into main motion. Passed.

Whoa. The substitution is better than the first attempt, but still it curtails staff rights.

Motion: Any staff member using the word "salve" is suspended the rest of the week.

Here we go.

Did not pass.

Okay, just a joke.

Motion: Take a recess for lunch at 3:15...

Motion: (5-30-10): Substitute "visitors to the Committee may only speak at the discretion of the JC Clerk" for "JC Clerk must give everyone directly involved in a case (plaintiffs, defendants) an opportunity to speak if it is requested by raising their hand," Passed.

They want to run more efficient meetings. We can live with this one.

Motion: Recess this meeting until 1:30 PM on May 12th, 2000. Passed.

Back to Order: 1:39 PM.

Motion: School Meeting Members (SMM) have the right to willfully withhold testimony from JC or Judicial School Meeting without being held in contempt. Passed.

Motion: No SMM may be brought before JC or JSM twice for the same incident. Passed.

Hello. This is almost "pleading the Fifth" and no double jeopardy? These are both good ideas.

Motion: To strike the law: "No one may infringe on anyone's right to freedom of expression, unless it directly violates someone's right to exist peaceably." Did not pass.

Motion: To amend the freedom of expression law to read: No one may infringe on anyone's right to freedom of expression, unless it is directed toward any demographic group or violates someone's right to exist peaceably." Passed.

Motion: To strike the freedom of expression law. Passed.

Motion: To informally discuss the situation. Passed.

Motion: Every SMM has the right to freedom of speech. Freedom of speech is defined by the ACLU. Did not pass.

Motion: To make the ACLU report "Freedom of Expression" Appendix A of the Fairhaven School Lawbook. Passed.

Motion: Every SMM has the right to freedom of expression as defined by Appendix A of the Lawbook. Passed.

Motion: To recess until 11:30AM, May 17th. Passed.

Substantive debate, reasonable conclusion, even a motion to discuss in the middle to brainstorm. Sounds like regular School Meeting.

...Back to Order 11:30 AM.

Motion: To reinstate 2-32-01, "Any motion which involves changing the school's lawbook may only be adopted after being read at one School Meeting, sitting for one week, then voted on again at the next regularly scheduled School Meeting." Did not pass.

Motion: To add "during which time it must be posted on the bulletin board." Passed.

Main Motion: To reinstate 2-32-01, "Any motion which involves changing the school's lawbook may only be adopted after being read at one School Meeting, sitting for one week, during which time it must be posted on the bulletin board, then voted on again at the next regularly scheduled School Meeting."

Motion: To adjourn. Passed.

When my colleagues and I met later to discuss our response to the "new rules," opinions varied. Would it be too subservient to accept the rules, to seize the opportunity to bridge the very real staff/teenager gulf? Or should we require second readings on each of their new proposals at the regular School Meeting?

We decided to defer to the letter of the law; their meetings were deemed legitimate the next day at School Meeting. The next year we hired Lisa, a founder of Evergreen Sudbury in Maine. She was shocked to discover the "student sponsor" rule on the books, although not observed in practice. Hearing her argument that she had come to work at a school that practiced equality, School Meeting struck the rule.

As for the spirit of the law, especially the need for transparency in a democracy, we carefully closed all the loopholes at the next School Meeting as well, making George and his gang's actions a one-time occurrence. But, oh, to have been in that room when they met! I remember the angst that led them to meet in secret, but I treasure their reasonableness once they did.

In the end, the best part of the story is not just what they did, it's what they did not do. They could have voted to fire me, to allow smoking on campus, or to deny younger students' rights, to name a few. Instead, they debated freedom of speech, finally appending the Lawbook. They had some fun, but they grew more serious as they combed through the lawbook, looking for ways to improve its contents and thereby their education, their school. All of our countercultural trust in children rang true in that closed room. This was no *Lord of the Flies*. "Your" lawbook became theirs.

Ever since we adopted these changes, once or twice a year, Law Clerks and interested parties have culled the school rules for passages that need amendment or deletion. The School Meeting has final say on each proposed change, often debating the finer points of the law in question prior to voting. The process keeps the document fresh; it also re-commits the community to the rule of law.

It's called "The Coup" by us old-timers. For years I have thought of it as George and his fellow students' final exam, a feat of diligence and empowerment. George has attended many alumni events in the years since The Coup. He's always helpful, quick to apologize for any trouble he may have caused, and expresses gratitude for the opportunity to attend Fairhaven.

This episode was also a crucial, early test for the Fairhaven staff and School Meeting. Recognizing, even accepting loop-holes affirms the importance of the Lawbook and the rule of law itself. Our acceptance of their quasi-legal action was like one nation recognizing the other, establishing the school culture as much as any dozen regular School Meetings, as much as one hundred JC cases.

Have we had any coups since May 2000? No, thankfully. Do teenagers at Fairhaven always feel empowered since then? No again, regretfully.

At yesterday's School Meeting, some thirty students came to vote among vying candidates for the essential positions of JC Clerks. We elected the winners by a one-vote margin. Later, we debated whether Maureen's dog Ruby could visit, the finer points of power tool certification, and new student attendance policies. Staff opinions varied as widely as student opinions. For perhaps the thousandth time since the coup, I absorbed the difficult experience of losing a vote, the real world lesson of not getting my way. Every time debate seemed at an end, Chloe, the student Chair, asked, "Is there any further discussion?" Seeing none, she called for a show of hands, and we all took the next steps, together, down this long, democratic road.

After the Flood

WINTER TEMPERATURES IN OUR MID-ATLANTIC region often hover at or near freezing, leading to at least one significant ice storm per year. In February, 2007 freezing rain sheathed local forests in ice, breaking limbs and felling trees, causing power outages all over the region. Fairhaven School lost its electricity for three days. When the power returned, a faulty sprinkler main that had frozen burst, flooding the new building on a Saturday with thousands of gallons of water, rendering it a construction site for the next month.

In true Fairhaven fashion, one neighbor, a parent of two alumni, followed the fire trucks and tried to salvage as many books as possible. Two students and one graduate also rushed in to help current and former staff members mere hours after the flood.

Gathering as staff in our sodden office the following Monday

morning was a grim experience; our newest and biggest building was soaked through and through. Furniture, carpets, books,
office supplies and equipment were damaged and beginning to
smell. The custom maple floorboards in the expansive Chesapeake Room were already cupping from their brief time under
water.

Staff members and students salvaged what we could those
first few days, piling less urgent objects on and under porches
and covering them with tarps, and hauling necessary items to
a temporary office in the dry old building. Two-thirds of our
space had become unusable overnight. Over the next month, as
we dried out, the school's culture and students passed a test of
resilience, accommodation, and resolve. So many of the quali-
ties we ascribe to Sudbury-educated students manifested themselves, describing the episode provides a case study.

Staff began the process, moving school systems like attendance sheets and JC record-keeping to new locations in the
old building. The Aesthetics Clerk and Committee anticipated
room uses and re-arranged accordingly. Ingenious members of
the Digital Arts Corporation set up the school's projector and
hung a sheet for movie viewing in the Activity Room. The Attendance Clerk softened the attendance requirements for the
first week after the flood.

As Official Authorities Clerk, I spent most of my time navi-
gating a second flood of insurance agents, insurance adjustors,
disaster restoration workers, and contractors. We became a testament to paying for a premium insurance policy, ending the
month with an improved building. Between calls and meetings,
I waded through the crowded building, absorbing the remarkable actions of our students.

Some perspective helps. Our original building has five
small to medium-sized rooms with doors that close, a kitchen,

a round, common room in the middle (the Circle Room), a bigger, open room (the Activity Room, where the students watched movies), and three bathrooms. Enter 85 people with no clear end in sight.

To a person, we entered with upbeat, positive attitudes. "I love this new Fairhaven!" one younger girl declared on Day One. Of course as time passed the novelty wore off. However, the positive attitudes did not. At Fairhaven, the ultimate measure of whether people are not getting along is the Judicial Committee. Although the Committee did have to invoke the "No dumpster diving" rule when some teenagers tried to reclaim damaged furniture for use by the stream (another story), never during that month was JC inundated by its own flood of fights, disagreements, or arguments. We simply abided one another.

Freedom to go outside proved essential during the protracted crisis. Imagine a conventional student body stuck inside during such a circumstance. During the flood month, students played more than the usual organized outdoor games—Capture the Flag, four square, basketball, hide and seek, and football. They also played countless games with no names—girls being horses, boys wrestling, younger students just running around. Older students took advantage of the school's open campus policy to leave during the busiest part of the day.

Freedom to relocate inside the building proved essential as well. Most days the Circle Room hosted four or five simultaneous conversations. Somebody would open a door to see whom they could write up for breaking the rule prohibiting loud noises in the building, only to find a general din. Freedom gave intolerance an escape valve. Too loud? Find somewhere else.

On cold days, sometimes there was nowhere else. Every room throbbed with activity and bodies. Porches and outside were too frigid. A conventional school would have ordered a temporary classroom immediately. The curriculum imperative. In the middle of the second week, staff and students vigorously debated whether we should demand a trailer from our insurance carrier. To some the bloom was off the rose: we were not conducting business as usual, and any other school would get a trailer. Yet many students were enjoying the togetherness as social groups rearranged through necessity and proximity generated new relationships and activities. They liked it. In the end, not getting a trailer prevailed, primarily because the insurance agent and contractors had worked overtime from day one. The end of reconstruction was in sight, and not insisting on a trailer would prove a valuable negotiating chip down the road.

A tour of campus on a day in Week Three follows. Video gamers occupy the Mears Room, doing their thing. The dust has settled from an earlier television reservation disagreement. Across the hall a group is plugging away at a difficult puzzle depicting a polar bear surrounded by monochromatic, soft pink snow and sky. Students and staff members have been working on it since the flood. When JC needs the table, they lay a cloth over the puzzle with much ceremony. The school's administrative assistant is working on a relocated office computer in the same room. Leaving this room for the entryway, one encounters a student inviting people to view her newly redecorated cubby. Now a mod apartment for her stuffed monkey, complete with wallpaper, it's fabulous.

In the Circle Room, many distinct groups occupy tables and couches. Some are knitting. A group of younger people are playing with a score of doe-eyed figurines. They are not quiet. The Law Clerk and a staff member are recruiting the steady stream of passersby to run for the next JC Clerks in the upcoming School Meeting elections. Three girls work on a laptop over the school's wireless network.

In the small, sunny room adjacent to the Circle Room, several students are selling massages, makeovers and hair styling. Three young girls tug hair and rub hands as one staff member gets a new look and a massage. She looks fabulous. Three teens are conversing over pizza in the kitchen. Someone's popcorn pops in the microwave. Movies have given way to storytelling in the Activity Room. One student is composing, then reading aloud a wacky tale about doppelganger versions of her friends in the packed room. Another draws magic marker scenes as the story evolves.

In the temporary office, the Aesthetics Clerk is searching for replacement furniture online. A colleague fields an admissions call, scheduling a tour of the school after we reoccupy the new building. The Bookkeeping Committee is meeting in the Art Room, sharing the space with a teenager painting dots onto her yearlong pointillist piece and a younger student building Plasticene models on a tray. An extension cord runs out the back door to the amplifier by the swing set where students blast rock and roll to the forest.

Back in the Activity Room, the story is on hold as the scribe has left for French class. Several older teens are reliving their youths, digging in the Lego bins to build models. Their nostalgic enthusiasm is contagious, a fitting end to this tour. For four weeks, we invent and reinvent activities, we deal with each other, and, yes, sometimes we pull out our hair! Mostly, we abide the circumstances.

Drastic change refreshes Fairhaven's culture. Once or twice each year the Computer Corporation closes school computers for maintenance. Several years ago, a charismatic older teen brought a motion to School Meeting to ban all screens for a week. The JC often imposes room or activity restrictions. Flood month was the Godzilla of such shake-ups, and has had lasting, salutary effects. School Meeting members of all ages deepened relationships. New interests and activities flourished. Staff members relearned their jobs from different perspectives.

School Meeting mandated a half hour of labor before each School Meeting member could return to the shiny new building. Pent-up energy and excitement produced a blizzard of furniture moving, unpacking in the new building and deep cleaning in the old building. We marveled at the new maple floor upstairs and the new carpet, paint and bookshelves downstairs. People tested the beefed up soundproofing between floors. In a classic vignette embodying Sudbury sense of time and conscience, a full month and a half after the cleaning day, I asked a graduating student who's a devoted old building denizen for help moving some boxes across a hall. Although I had no idea he hadn't fulfilled his obligation yet, he got up from his laptop, saying, "Well, I still need to do that thirty minutes, so I guess I'll do it now," and promptly left the old building for the first time since the flood.

Just after a student placed the last piece of the formidable polar bear puzzle, and just before our annual fundraising Gala, we reclaimed the reconstructed new building with gusto, needing its spacious rooms after a very tight month. Like my box mover, some refused at first to leave the old building. We all looked back at its trusty confines with fond respect, its ample legend one chapter thicker. The Little Building That Hosted 85 One February. Back to normal, many yearn for those crowded days. So fond are they of the togetherness, two girls have brought a motion to School Meeting, hoping to declare Flood Week a school tradition each year. Amend it to Flood Day, and they've got my vote.

What We're Made Of

When the flood jams us all together,
we become subatomic particles,
protons banging their drums,

neutrons watching from the couch.
Nuclear power charges when a blizzard
closes the doors. Each bounces

off the other, first creating heat
then breaking off, attracted to the quiet
new girl over by the window watching

electrons orbit the building,
their mass so light, their feet barely
print the snow.

The Munchkins: A Case Study

AN ENTERPRISING SIX-YEAR-OLD once sponsored legislation to allow running in the Chesapeake Room on Fridays. On many Fridays, the sounds of footfalls audible in the office below achieve a rhythm, a repetitious sameness that can mean only one thing: Munchkin practice. Arising from the mists in the first few years, the Munchkins seem to predate the school. Perhaps the most accurate analog for them is junior Amazons, the legendary race of female warriors from antiquity.

My earliest recollection of the Munchkins is a war the all-girl army prosecuted against some hapless boys early in the school's history. There was much pre-war negotiating of ground rules, tons of training and strategizing, and a couple of brief skirmishes of actual fighting on the field. The war produced a few JC cases, but JC dropped these because everybody had agreed to the ground rules. Despite their martial origin, the modern Munchkins have become integrated into the school culture. It's been years since they have actually battled an opponent, although one can imagine them rising to the challenge.

While the battles have entered Fairhaven history, the training continues. They set up jumps and obstacle courses, and then, for hours at a time, the elected leaders put them through their paces. Weather permitting, they train outside. Sometimes the jumps and obstacles are stacked folding chairs in the Chesapeake Room. Lately, the look of training has paralleled Munchkin interest in horseback riding. Perhaps they've become a cavalry.

Once a year, a Munchkin practice involves more than the usual amount of sitting and talking. Then people begin voting: it's time to elect a queen and a vice-queen. In early years, these elections took place in a crowded bathroom. Subsequent votes have been held outside. No mere elections, they involve both candidate speeches and some form of multi-voting. When the most recent queen opted not to run, her throne was hotly contested.

To my knowledge, the Munchkins are an entirely oral society. Aside from rare references in JC Reports, there's no mention of them in any school documents, nor do they record minutes of their meetings or decisions. Yet for many of their membership, their activities seem to be among the most important in their Fairhaven experience.

Although they elected one or two boys into their number years ago, the Munchkins have been primarily a female tribe. New girls join, older ones fade back into the larger cultural matrix of the school. Explicitly physical and democratic, with a smattering of ecological philosophy, Munchkin training is a unique hybrid with classical similarities.

Both an extended form of play and a vitally serious sub-culture for its membership, the Munchkins exemplify Fairhaven education. First, they have an extremely physical component. Their training sessions are real workouts that occur on a regular basis. On more than one occasion, I've heard Munchkins talking about sore legs after practice (not complaining, by the way, just identifying the fact of sore legs). As a form of exercise, Munchkin training evolves, moving to higher jumps, longer balance beam walking, or new obstacle courses.

Second, it is a created model. A Fairhaven experience is expressly dynamic. Throughout their history, the Munchkins have changed. One year they started making birdcalls to communicate across the campus in relative secrecy. Somewhere along the line they began meeting at "the fairy tree," an evocative, spreading willow oak on the western edge of campus. They seem to have developed a significant environmental ethic sitting in its copious shade. The paradox of the Munchkins occurs in all play at Fairhaven—they know they're playing, and at the same time they take it very seriously as they do it. We see this in computer gaming, sports, playing house, and numerous other forms of play (read Daniel Greenberg for more on play).

Third, it is bound by democratic practice. Although exclusive membership and dictatorial leadership—she is a queen after all—have sullied the Munchkins from time to time, their hybrid monarchy/democracy has been a laboratory for many School Meeting members. What should be the limits of power? What are a person's qualifications to lead? Should she still enforce the rule requiring Munchkins to not wear shoes? Is it fair to restrict membership by vote? Many a Munchkin who cast her first votes under the fairy tree later votes with ease in School Meeting.

Although the Munchkins have had the advantage of staying

power and public activities, scores of similar subcultures have existed on campus. We have hosted the LDs, the skateboarders, the chamber of nerds, the paper gamers, and many, many more that may remain nameless threads in the school's rainbow fabric. Each subculture becomes part of the school's history and part of each student's individual growth and education.

So many elements go into a student's experience, we sometimes explain a Fairhaven education by what it's not: no compulsory curriculum, no report cards, no principal, and so on. This brief description of the Munchkins may offer a glimpse of what a Fairhaven education is. Fairhaven School is a place where each student is physically and intellectually free to choose her own settings, constrained only by the democratic decisions made by the majority.

Without a Net:
Staffing at Fairhaven

ON ONE PARTICULAR DAY in early October a staff member at
Fairhaven was debating why the Judicial Committee should
refer three defendants to School Meeting. His cell phone was
on, as he was awaiting a call back from the insurance agent.
A student rushed into the meeting, declaring, "Tommy is hurt
real bad and you need to come." Her pale face and scared eyes
pulled him out of his seat and the debate. En route to the office,
he got a substitute staff for JC. Heading down the stairs, a student pleaded with him to play football. Not now. After taking
the injured student to get stitches on her seesaw-split chin, he
returned to campus, just in time for a parent conference with
yet another student who's nervous about getting referred to
School Meeting. Referred? He remembered the earlier JC case.

After the successful conference, he discovered the JC decision he had to leave—no referral. Exercising his rights and wanting to complete his interrupted argument at School Meeting, he filed an appeal. After checking his messages for the insurance call, he left the office, looking for a young man with a football.

Staffing at Fairhaven and other Sudbury schools offers as many challenges and rewards as any educational job out there. The analogies multiply: surfing a tidal wave, pushing a boulder up a mountain, skydiving, playing in a jazz combo. Days can be remarkably challenging, variable and sublime. Working at Fairhaven qualifies as a vocation, not just a job.

To distinguish both the school and its employees from traditional schools, Fairhaven adopted Sudbury Valley's nomenclature, calling its faculty "staff members" rather than "teachers." Staff at Fairhaven can play both the administrative and teaching roles found in other schools, but they also wear a variety of other hats throughout each day. Staff can be mentors and role models, coaches and mediators, leaders and listeners, artists and judges. In the end, the roles are only limited by vocabulary, so perhaps sketching examples will enhance this description.

One of my colleagues is a twenty-something artist. He manages the building and grounds. Fairhaven's twelve acres and two sizable buildings require ongoing maintenance, so he's always fixing something—doors, light fixtures, maybe a ceiling tile. Because of his obligations and his personal style, he's seldom in the office. When he's dealing with a repair he attracts students. One year students approached him about building tables, including one young man who wanted to build a giraffe table for his mother. They spent weeks on the large covered deck designing, constructing and painting what became two connected pieces. An exemplar of the artistic sensibility, he draws whenever he attends the many meetings at school.

As the youngest staff member, he's always up for a game of basketball or Frisbee. Last year the School Meeting elected him Attendance Clerk, a deliberately administrative assignment to counterbalance his "fun staff" status.

One of Fairhaven's founders was a staff and parent who had worked for years with pre-schoolers. School Meeting voted her Aesthetics Clerk, so she had the daunting task of managing both the appearance and cleanliness of the buildings. She spent much of her time cleaning, organizing cleaners, and strategizing new cleaning plans. So far, the lifespan of any cleaning solution seems never to exceed six months. School Meeting also voted her into the position of Registrar. She read to younger students and frequently gave voice to their perspective in JC and School Meeting. She also brought her interests into the school, including singing, yoga, and storytelling. She helped create the Field Trip Corporation and took countless students to various interesting places. She specialized in parent communication, creating it as a clerkship.

In the early days, we hired a quiet mother of two of our young students. She soon cemented her role at school when she assumed responsibility for the computer network. With a background in the sciences, she also became our default higher math instructor. A pianist, she taught some music theory and piano over her tenure. In contrast to the omnipresent building manager, she spent much of her time either in the office or working with individuals or pairs of students. She co-created the Computer Corporation with many self-described "geeks." This weekly meeting served dual functions: practical management of the school's computer infrastructure and laboratory for democratic decision-making and group work. When she decided not to run for staff a few years ago, the School Meeting retained her as our bookkeeper.

I could write a lengthy exposition for every one of my colleagues from Fairhaven's first decade. We have attracted many interesting, knowledgeable, diligent staff members, and each finds his or her own clerkships and style. Each year the School Meeting must assign responsibilities by electing Clerks. Although the school has both experienced staff and new staff, our structure has no boss per se. The Staff Hiring Committee and ultimately School Meeting decide all aspects of working at Fairhaven by vote. Who will do the administrative heavy lifting? Who will do the literal heavy lifting? Do we have somebody who can teach the academic basics? Who's the computer person? And so on with all the categories of accountability we call clerkships.

Yet nobody works here merely for clerkships. Relationships with free young people are the magnetic force that attracts adults and retains them. We staff members must check in with the students, read them, read to them, play with them, and challenge them. One of our most important jobs is to be straight with the students, to "call them as we see them." A successful staff member can recognize and bridge the seeming gulf between tolerating the students' free choices and articulating our opinions about these choices.

Say a staff member sees a new student, self conscious and socially uncertain, coming on way too strong with his peers. Most recognize that saying something the first day would be out of bounds, and most also recognize that saying nothing is too laissez-faire. The interaction of interpersonal skill and experience that informs when to challenge the student on his sometimes annoying behavior (his abuse of his freedom) defines staffing at Fairhaven. Crucially, a bedrock of friendliness and trust must ground the staff-student relationship to allow the more difficult conversation.

Or perhaps a teenager is attending school less and less. Her relationships at school are becoming tenuous. You miss her piano playing, and you're concerned for her emotional well being. Staff members are attracted to the school's acceptance of each individual's educational process. When is the time to intervene, to directly confront the teenager with your concerns? The school has mechanisms for addressing shoddy attendance (including JC cases, letters home, and School Meeting referral and removal) and these provide formal opportunities for commentary. What if her attendance is borderline, but you still have concerns?

One of the most helpful rules of thumb for Sudbury staffing is the following: if you would say it to a peer, say it to the student. Being candid with our students is absolutely a bedrock trait. Every one of us has a different communication style with our students, but we must remain engaged with the student body and open to improving our level of engagement with each student and with the student body as a whole. However, we would seldom approach a peer outside of school with an abstract agenda: "Gosh, Jane, you should spend more time reading chapter books."

Absent the traditional school formula for feedback (curriculum, report card, standardized tests), staff members play a vital role in the successful growth and development of the students. We are hired to be steady and willing adults in the community. In the school's second year, David asked for my support at School Meeting. He wanted permission to build a fort. "I'll support you," I said, since I agreed with his motion, "but I only have one vote."

"Yes, but you have lots of influence. People listen to you." Rarely have I heard such a succinct summation of one of the role of staff at Fairhaven. The challenge comes in using this influence judiciously.

Balance characterizes Fairhaven staffing. For every successful intervention or use of influence, each of us has far more examples of staying out of the way. As the adults in the community, we must model trust in the students. Trusting them is the
bread and butter that sets the table for the occasional gourmet
meal. A staff member must come around the corner at school
with a practiced habit of acceptance, yet remain prepared to
register objection. Being okay with "hanging out" enables the
deep conversation with a student who may be stuck in process.
Feeling comfortable with students playing House permits the
staff member to write up students who may be running while
playing the game.

No aspect of staffing is formulaic. The "boss" is a weekly
School Meeting that votes. The clerkships are areas of responsibility (bookkeeping, building, admissions, etc.) that we must
cover to the best of our abilities. We teach classes according to
student request, our level of expertise and experience, and room
in our schedule. We interact informally with students and colleagues when we can. Experienced colleagues advise rookies.

Clerkships are tangible, measurable aspects of our jobs.
Did you pay the bills? Is that door still sticking? Have you responded to all of the admissions queries? They are often huge
tasks, works in progress that staff members have to learn to put
down in order to be available to students. Sometimes we have
to schedule "hanging out" because other commitments suck up
our time. Some days we drift throughout the campus, checking in with people; on other days we may plant ourselves in a
central location so folks can find us. Always, though, we tread
lightly, careful to balance (that word again) availability with respectful distance.

Evaluation of staff occurs on many levels—students will tell you how you're doing, colleagues will do the same in conversation or at monthly staff meetings, and School Meeting debate and decisions will offer guidance. This year we initiated a midyear written evaluation, and the Staff Hiring Committee continues to brainstorm strategies for evaluation. Still, the ultimate evaluation is the annual staff election.

Fairhaven School has no tenured faculty. Rather, each of us, from brand new employees to founders, must be re-hired each May. A staff candidate must first be nominated from the floor of School Meeting. Next, each candidate must receive at least fifty percent "yes" votes in a secret ballot election in which each School Meeting member (each current staff member and students) has a vote. Finally, the Staff Hiring Committee proposes a slate of candidates from the pool. The number of days for which staff are hired must conform to what's available in next year's budget. A special School Meeting debates this slate, often amending it prior to passage.

The three-week long election season—from the first person nominating someone, through the student Elections Clerk posting the results, to the School Meeting's final vote to adopt a slate—distinguishes Fairhaven and other Sudbury schools both for its arduousness and for its ultimate affirmation. Representing the ultimate in accountability, this multi-step democratic hiring process can be both honest and secretive, intimidating and rewarding. Since the final meetings can finish with hurt feelings and an exhausted staff, we are open to changing the process by democratic vote in the future. Slate debates take place on a Friday to enable staff to totter home and go to bed. To date, we remain committed to placing this crucial task—hiring the staff—in the hands of the entire community.

Staffing at Fairhaven is like whitewater rafting. Who can

mend a slow leak? How's the integrity of the whole raft? Should we hit that standing wave head-on or paddle left? Teamwork and communication steady the course. Some lucky days we get to drift downstream. Sunlight dries the latest rapids from our faces. Our passengers are all paddling along as we admire the timeless cliff walls we're passing.

.

The Role of Parents

IN JULY 1998, Sudbury Valley trustee and contractor Alan White
and I were taking a break from hammering nails in Fairhaven
School's first building. As we admired the forest through the
opening that would become the shop window, I asked if he had
any advice for when we actually opened the school at the end
of the summer. Alan thought a long moment, finally looking
up from beneath the straw hat he wore for the entire project.
"You've got to reassure the parents. Talk to them, listen to them.
Make sure they understand the school."

Cogent advice, although not the easiest to follow. If students
are our clients, then parents are their sponsors, absolutely as
necessary as the young people themselves in a school supported entirely by tuition. Parents drop off their children at the cir-

cular driveway every day, enabling the singular education that is Fairhaven. Beyond driving their children, what role do parents play in a Sudbury school? After ten years, some guidelines have emerged.

Do Your Homework
Every year, families contact the school, sometimes telling us they've been thinking about enrolling for years. Hooray! Because what we do is so different from traditional school, children whose parents have thought long and hard about Fairhaven before enrolling tend to flourish. They have read about Sudbury schooling, both on our website and other schools' websites. They have read SVS books. They know as much as possible about what they're getting themselves into.

Ask the Hard Questions
We interview every prospective family at least twice, both at the beginning of a visiting week and at the end. In this process, no question should be out of bounds. How do you ensure safety? Will my daughter learn to read? Is there bullying at Fairhaven? How do you provide for interests beyond staff expertise? Where does he keep his belongings? What do I tell his old school? How will my son do if he wants to go to college? These and countless other questions are not only appropriate; we expect them. Families that don't ask questions can be less satisfied than families that do.

Let Your Child Own Her Education
We recommend that new parents allow their children to become established on campus. We've even asked more than one eventual colleague to wait an entire school year before petitioning School Meeting to volunteer, to substitute, or to run for staff.

Although this may seem at odds with the conventional wisdom of traditional schools that solicit heavy parental involvement from day one, experience supports this strategy. We are fostering individual student agency, and early parental presence can inhibit this process.

Talk To Staff
We encourage parents to talk to us, on philosophical as well as practical matters. Call the office with questions about the ice skating trip. Approach staff members in the parking lot at the end of the day about how School Meeting makes a decision. Because our policy is to discuss students when they are present, a staff member with whom parents are chatting may suggest a conference if the conversation begins to focus on their child's behavior. We also arrange conferences upon parental request, both to discuss specific concerns or more general questions about their child's progress at Fairhaven.

Synchronize Your Home with the School
We encourage families to consciously try to replicate Fairhaven's freedom and responsibility at home. Families who succeed at this have held family meetings, and have limited interventions regarding how children spend their time as much as possible. Although we are reluctant to tell people how to operate their households, students whose transition between home and school is relatively seamless tend to thrive.

Support the School's Decisions
Perhaps School Meeting has voted to change the guidelines regarding Internet usage and a student disagrees with the decision. Maybe School Meeting has suspended a child. Parent support of these and other decisions is crucial. If a young stu-

dent comes home with a tale of unbelievable injustice, we urge parents to check with staff before getting upset. As staff who are also parents, we have all too often witnessed first-hand incidents at school becoming somewhat exaggerated in the telling at home.

Moreover, unlike students at other schools, students at Fairhaven often have the ability to try to reverse decisions they don't like at subsequent meetings. While we advise supporting the school's decision, we also advise parents to clarify their child's options in the democratic process. Remind them of their unique access to power. Encourage them to go to the next Computer Corporation meeting and make their case for Internet access.

Participate in the Democratic Process

After their child has been enrolled for two months, parents become voting members of the School Assembly, the policy-making body of Fairhaven School. Assembly membership includes all parents, staff members, and students in addition to elected public members (usually interested alumni and former parents). All Assembly members may make motions for the agenda, and all receive written notice of Assembly meetings. Those who choose to attend can discuss and vote on substantive issues, including the annual budget, staff salary policies, and graduation policies.

Embody Trust in Your Children

Parents who send their children to Fairhaven School constitute a remarkable group. Independent, courageous, and thoughtful, they have made the school what it is today in numerous ways. They have built the school both by driving nails and participating in scores of meetings over the years. Most importantly, they have built the school by sending us their children. This simple act—enrollment—is a leap of faith and trust that their child can and will prepare themselves to succeed in the world.

Parents of successful students maintain this trust for the duration of their enrollment. Do they have questions? Do they have concerns from time to time? Of course they do. When their child struggles, these parents reinforce the school philosophy with their own belief in their child. "I know this is difficult, but you're smart and capable of doing it" is a very empowering thing for a student to hear.

Conversely, some parents have chosen to arrange outside tutoring in academic areas, "just to keep up." The message this sends the child is, "We know what's best for you to do at school, and when you should be doing it. We don't trust you to figure it out on your own and make it happen." Student-requested instruction in dance, math, drumming, or reading? Absolutely. The practice students get in repeatedly figuring out what they want to do and going for it when they're ready builds character.

The difference between the school providing help or instruction when students want it, as compared to parents requiring progress in certain areas may well be the difference between a successful Fairhaven experience and a mediocre one, between a child who feels confident about her own judgement and a child who needs adult direction and approval.

We recognize the challenge the school can represent for parents, and, for their children's sake, we encourage them to take it on. Fairhaven's annals overflow with examples of the amazing results when parents let go, and we are here to hold their hands as they do so. Putting on Alan's straw hat, we are always here to help parents understand the school.

...But Children Need Structure

No misunderstanding about Fairhaven is more commonplace than the idea that the school has no structure. Consider a sample Monday for Chloe. She arrives around ten-thirty and goes to her piano lesson with Kim at 11:30. At noon she chairs a JC meeting since she is an alternate Clerk and the JC clerk, is absent. She has a late lunch at 2 o'clock during the weekly JC Clerks meeting with the Law Clerk. At 2:30 she heads downstairs to join the Yearbook Committee working in front of a computer. For the rest of her day, she chills with friends, signing out to go home at 4:48, twelve minutes before the day's end.

Meetings form the spine of the school. First, the two basics: JC daily, School Meeting on Wednesdays at one. Then, longstanding regulars: Kitchen Corp. on Fridays at eleven; Computer Corp. Thursdays at eleven; Music Corp. Thursdays at 2:30; Field Trip Corp. every Monday at noon; Theater Corp. Tuesdays at eleven-thirty. This year students and staff have also arranged math, creative writing, reading, French, and photography classes.

Every meeting at school has its own internal structure, from the very formal School Meeting to a low-key Friday math class where we play cards. Meetings that transact business do so by majority vote.

Crucially, Fairhaven's intricate network of structure is not compulsory. We have two basic requirements: record your attendance and serve on JC for two weeks. In addition, JC or School Meeting may, at times, require your attendance.

So, yes, students can and do fashion their own days on campus. Many spend less time in meetings than Chloe, a busy teen. Some will assume roles like hers as they grow. Maybe they will choose one or two corporations to call home. Still others will live their school life playing, talking, building relationships one day at a time, aware of the structures surrounding them, yet blissfully free to create their lives in the manner they choose.

Father Figures

The boy whose father died last June rushed into school
    to thrash the drums,
each frantic beat spraying sheetrock with black and
    blood red drips.

He had stepped to me last fall, when mine died. Most
    young men,
like I would have, avoided my shiny eyes. He looked
    at me, he touched.

So he sought me after the stroke took his pop. His lean
    frame
pulsed with sobs as we embraced, our chests striking
    one another.

He boxes now, relying on others to lace his gloves three
    days a week.
He's painted his combat boots white, like Ali's at the
    Thrilla in Manila.

Time has toughened our hugs to a handshake, faded
    his drumbeats to jazz.
His wrist cracks from all the punching. We squeeze
    harder, men. When our eyes lock,

I can hear a starlit porch chat on Jefferson, then Whitman
    with his dad, Dan,
who wore a Navy tattoo and packed gourmet lunches
    —summer sausages, Bartlett pears,
who daily wrote Jared across the full brown bags.

The Importance of Talking Trash II

Marvin's mother had signed him up for Fairhaven's summer school, our annual three weeks of freedom and responsibility on a smaller scale. When he arrived to discover he was the oldest by a few significant years, Marvin's face sank. "What am I going to do with these guys?" he asked, glaring at the clump of pre-teen boys gabbing about computers.

"You'll be all right," I said, slapping five with Marvin. I knew we shared a passion for sports, and that the two of us would spend hours together. "How's Ravens summer camp going?"

"Well, Ray Lewis didn't have to go to jail, so our defense should be as good as usual."

"Not as good as the Redskins," I volleyed my standard Marvin provocation, resuming our ongoing trash talking. Fairhaven School is more in Washington Redskins country, but attracts plenty of diehard Baltimore Ravens fans, none as purple and black as Marvin.

"The Redskins," Marvin could only laugh. "They haven't won anything since George Bush's father was president." Touché.

And so we bantered those few weeks, often tossing a football back and forth. Once or twice a day the younger boys joined us, and we softened our throws to include them before they scampered back to their games. Mostly, it was just the two of us. He preferred it that way, both because he couldn't tolerate his ball getting scuffed when the younger boys dropped it and because he wanted my undivided attention.

When he had arrived at Fairhaven a year before, Marvin had almost no discernible sense of humor. Perhaps the most literal person I'd met, he could not grasp the nuances of humor and talking trash. A hyper-social environment, Fairhaven was a perfect match for his needs.

After a week of football, I broke out my Frisbee. "I suck at Frisbee," *he said, dropping my first throw to him.*

"You sure do," I said. I couldn't resist, chasing his wild toss. Anger flashed for a second across his eyes, then a smile of recognition. What a difference a year makes.

Marvin improved his Frisbee throwing on a rapid curve. Within a week, he was quite good at both catching and throwing. He bought his own green disc and we used it in the circle driveway. Whenever the boys approached, he put it away, again concerned not to damage the Frisbee on the asphalt. Sometimes, though, he would relent, doling out the same patience with the beginners I had shown him earlier.

When school resumed that fall, Marvin joined the avid Frisbee crowd with confidence. Nods of acceptance and assent greeted his first throws. He became a valued player in our competitive Ultimate Frisbee games, often the person who liked to go long to catch the scoring throws. After the games, there he'd be, dishing out the trash or taking it, comfortable in the matrix of humor and communication.

Never a Dull Moment

THIRTEEN-YEAR-OLD Malcolm wrote the following motion on the School Meeting agenda:

Move: My vote counts for 1,000 votes. (Malcolm)

As often happens, my colleagues and I talked about the motion before Wednesday at one o'clock. Was this a joke? Was Malcolm, who happened to be a professional actor, just playing a part? Or did he seriously want to transform Fairhaven's robust, hard-won democracy into a dictatorship? Fellow staff members and other students were not sure.

At least half the student body packed the large Chesapeake Room that Wednesday. After we transacted JC business and old business, Malcolm's provocative motion came to the floor. A buzz electrified the room. Looking around the crowd, I was not clear who had come to support Malcolm's ascendancy and who had come to oppose it. Gulp.

At the front of the room, Chloe, the School Meeting Chair, conferred with Kim, a staff member and the elected Secretary. Kim raised her hand, and after Chloe called on her, she addressed the throng: "Look, this motion is out of order. Both the Assembly and Fairhaven School, Inc. established Fairhaven as a democratic school. One person, one vote."

Malcolm shot his hand up. "I would only do things that are good for the school," he began.

Chloe cut him off. "What Kim is saying is that this motion is out of order. That means we cannot hear it at all at School Meeting. Even if we wanted to, we don't have the authority to make your vote count for one thousand votes."

"Who does have the authority?" asked Malcolm.

"Only the Assembly could grant you one thousand votes," Chloe replied. "But it would be a really bad idea and it would probably never happen."

"How do I call an Assembly meeting?" Malcolm, the boy who would be king, continued. The room grew restless.

"I'll talk to you after School Meeting, but I agree with Chloe," said Kim, one of the people who had voted at Fairhaven School's first organizational meeting some fifteen years earlier, and who had been raising her hand as one vote ever since. "This is a really bad idea."

When Chloe announced the next order of business, two-thirds of the people in the room left. Many smiled, pleased that tyranny had been vanquished.

After School Meeting, a straight-faced Malcolm got all the particulars from Kim regarding making a motion at the school Assembly. Another colleague, who could not stand the notion of a de facto dictator any longer, grilled Malcolm on why on earth he would make such a motion. He continued to play it straight. I left for the old building.

Avi, one of Malcolm's peers, greeted me with a JC Grievance form in hand. "I'm writing up Malcolm for Preamble. What do you think?" he asked. Avi, who wears tie dyed T-shirts every day, beckoned me to join him at a table.

What did I think? I thought Malcolm and Avi are business rivals, both selling food concessions to a limited market. I also thought Avi might not mind seeing Malcolm's heretofore clean JC record tarnished. I sat down anyway. "He has the right to make any motion he wants at School Meeting. What's your allegation?" I asked.

"Well, I was offended by the idea of him having a thousand votes. It made me uncomfortable," he began. "But this isn't about the motion itself. Apparently, Malcolm was bribing people with chocolate chip cookies to come vote for his motion. Maybe even cash." He looked up from filling in the form. "Don't you think that's a violation of Preamble?"

"I do, if it's true. I'll join your complaint," I said, thinking, here we go again: blowback. According to Webster's, "an unintended adverse reaction or effect from an action or cause, especially political."[9] We eased into the rush of the Fairhaven stream.

Building our case for the next day, Avi and I questioned each School Meeting member who passed through the Circle Room. Did Malcolm offer you cookies? What for? Did you take them? Our list of bribe recipients grew. We followed a lead to discover that one young man had been looking for two dollars for pizza money. Hearing this, Malcolm offered him the two dollars if he came to vote for his motion. The case thickened. Staff wondered how kids who supposedly treasure their freedom were willing to sell it so cheaply. Or did they see it as a joke?

Knowing that Malcolm was distraught that we were bringing him to JC, and endangering his pristine record, I approached him the next day before the case. "You know, I think this may have all started as a joke," I began. "If so, that may be your best defense." Nothing from Malcolm. Man, he'll make a great poker player. "Was it a joke?"

"It may have been a joke," was all he said. I resisted the surprisingly strong urge to tell him I'd see him in court.

The JC deliberated over the case for about a half hour. Malcolm's defense was vigorous. He spent a fair amount of time defending his right to make the motion. Once the JC clarified that allegations of bribery were at issue, not his motion, he still had a strategy. He claimed that he was exercising his right to free speech. He compared his homemade cookies to campaign buttons in the larger community. He stressed that every School Meeting member, cookie recipient or not, had always been free to vote as they wished.

At issue was the following clause of our Lawbook's Preamble:

By freely joining this democratic community, every School Meeting member becomes responsible for its free and democratic atmosphere, and for its continued existence and well-being.

Persuading people to come support your motion? Yes. Offering them goods or cash? No. Deciding that bribery undermined the school's free and democratic atmosphere, with two members abstaining, JC voted to charge Malcolm with violating the school's Preamble. Julie, one the JC Clerks, spoke to Malcolm prior to his plea. "Look, we know you didn't break this rule deliberately, and we're only going to sentence you with a warning. How do you plead?"

Without hesitation, Malcolm pleaded not guilty, exercising his right to make his case at School Meeting. Upon hearing the same arguments and counter-arguments five days later, the larger group at School Meeting upheld the JC's decision to find Malcolm guilty of violating the Preamble.

Stinging from the stain on his record, Malcolm moved to expel himself! Various School Meeting members sprang to his defense, citing his clean record and his unique value to the school community. We discussed the need for "legal precedent" concerning any future allegations of bribery. At last, over Malcolm's dramatic protests, we issued him a warning. Never a dull moment.

The Playing Fields of Fairhaven

A TEN-YEAR-OLD GIRL is traversing the campus, poking her head into each room or group of young people, making the same announcement over and over: "We're playing blob tag on the field in five minutes." A group of students gathers later to play the invented game. Its rules are lost on me, but the pattern of students playing a wide variety of games is so commonplace it bears commentary. Going all the way back to the co-op days, Fairhaven students have played games, and we assume it is an activity we will always see at school.

In colder months, eventually somebody breaks out a deck of cards. Students have played War and Go Fish, and sometimes Solitaire. Older students teach one another how to play Spades and Hearts. Cribbage picked up steam one year, after a student made herself a cribbage board in the shop. Teenage girls seem to favor speed games like Spit in the Ocean, Egyptian Ratscrew (bequeathed to Fairhaven from Evergreen Sudbury School), or Speed. One winter we held a Hearts tournament, complete with official score sheets and a commissioner to calculate the standings. Aside from being fun and mathematical, playing cards provides a platform for conversation. Card players are not just becoming better card players, they are developing personae.

Sticking with the table games, students have played hours of chess on campus. Devotees know who's the best and newcomers with aspirations make challenges. These games can attract quite a crowd of onlookers. A staff member brought his interest in the Japanese strategy game, Go, to school where it retains a fervent following. Countless board games have covered our tables, including Monopoly, Parcheesi, and Risk. Magic Cards are extremely popular among the pre-teen boys.

Fairhaven students have been on the leading edge of computer and video gaming since we opened. From Madden football to Mario Cart, from RPGs to FPSs, our students play screen games with abandon and skill. As befits a generational shift, some parents and staff question these games, seeking, perhaps, reassurance as much as comprehension. Recently the majority of computer gaming has been online. Different patterns exist. Some people play for months, maybe years on end, and then get sick of the activity. Others play video or computer games as a deliberate, ongoing strategy to relieve stress. Some of our young people are quite serious in their aspirations to join the multi-billion dollar gaming industry. Achieving mastery is an absolute priority for most of the people who play. Many students play these games more heavily upon arriving at Fairhaven, as it offers a familiar milieu.

Googlers and developmental psychology students can find

extensive argumentation both for and against computer gaming. In the Computer Corporation and at School Meeting, we have engaged the debate for years. Two younger colleagues have been gamers themselves, which has proven very helpful for people like me who are all thumbs with the controllers, more at home with playing cards than a Gameboy. To date, we remain committed to the freedom of our students to engage in any activity for as long as they wish, provided they are in compliance with the Lawbook. The gamers continue.

Meanwhile, students may also be playing outside on our courts and fields. Many different team sports have been popular, including kickball, soccer, touch football, and Ultimate Frisbee. Games are usually co-ed, and players span a wide variety of ages and abilities. At a conference at Sudbury Valley School, where foursquare is king, a Fairhaven staff member's son got hooked, coming home with a mission. That fall, the Grounds Clerk painted a permanent foursquare court onto our parking lot. Basketball has been a constant. One year we happened to have enough boys aged ten and eleven to field a team, complete with uniforms and coaches. The Cougars' brief season had four road games that proved to be great fun for the players and their fans.

New players often sharpen their skills before joining the actual games. Sometimes critical mass for a game doesn't gather, and folks will just play catch or kick the soccer ball. Basketballers without enough people for a game may play Horse, Thirty-one, or Knockout. Our egalitarian setting serves the newcomers well, and there always seems to be room for one more player.

A gigantic pile of freshly-shredded bark mulch was dumped by a local arborist in a shady spot next to the circle. The Grounds Clerk, would later use it to cover bare patches and soften the playground area. Almost immediately, the under-teenage boy crowd occupied the fragrant mound and began playing King of the Hill. They grappled and shoved all day, and most of the next week. Like many at Fairhaven, the game was self-correcting, producing zero JC write-ups. This subset at school has played different versions of this game over the years, and it has always involved extended physical contests. Sometimes they have sticks; sometimes they wrestle.

Speaking of sticks, a few students with training in fencing brought the game of stick fighting to a whole new level one year when they brought various wooden swords and staffs to campus. After a couple of whacked hands and one whacked head, the School Meeting insisted the participants wear protective gear. Nevertheless, they sparred and parried their way across campus for some time, often attracting an audience.

The patterns are quite consistent. A small group of people begins a game at school. Others might know the game or have no reservations about learning on the fly. These players jump right in. Others may need to watch; they may ask questions or seek tips. Sooner or later, they pick up the wooden sword or the stick, or they line up to play ball. The lines between expert and novice may be clear or fuzzy, but the willingness to share knowledge seems to be an absolute. Our student body is smaller than most schools, so players tend to be motivated to create more players. We are also unbound by the exclusionary, competitive nature of mainstream school sports. We do not have tryouts and cuts, and although people play to win, competition does not predominate. Furthermore, since Fairhaven's educational paradigm is so egalitarian, eschewing the traditional boundaries, people learn things quickly here, from whoever seems to know more.

Capture the Flag is perhaps the quintessential Fairhaven team sport. Any age can play, and often does, from five-year-olds to adults. Players can choose their level of participation and their place on the field—the game requires and indeed values sprinters and jail guards, line holders and battlefield strategists. Hours may pass between captured flags. The annual, whole campus Capture the Flag game has become a Fairhaven School tradition, the highlight of the Alumni cookout for both current and returning students (and more than one returning parent).

Perhaps no category of gaming at Fairhaven shines quite like the invented games. Early on, two sisters brought their neighborhood game of Scientists and Monkeys to school, in which two sides competed, making nasty potions in the kitchen, then hiding them. Both the scientists and the monkeys ran across campus, chasing and hiding, constructing elaborate plans. Losers, I think, had to drink the other side's potion.

One year the Munchkin queen tied a long string to a full plastic water bottle. Standing in one spot, she spun the strung bottle in a circle, creating a moving target for her tribe. They watched it come, then leaped up to avoid it. In the game, if the bottle hits your foot, you're out until the next round. Thus, the birth of the bottle game. The queen got tired, and very dizzy, so others occupied the center. Non-Munchkins joined the game. People tried to time their jumps like entering a moving jump rope game. Speeds varied, rules evolved. The bottle game remains a fixture.

Fairhaven has a fine swing set—twelve feet tall, with galvanized poles and four swings. Very Old School. One day I looked out from the Art Room to see four swingers and a long line of students to one side, waiting their turn to run the gauntlet between the moving swings. Some crawled, and some ran. Winners made it all the way through without being touched by a swing or a swinger's outstretched foot. Named for a video game, this is Frogger.

At least once a season I'll arrive at school to see students busy in the driveway circle, where they're sweeping, negotiating, and creating their wares. They have subdivided their "town" by marking the blacktop with chalk or stone-scratched drawings. The Shop game is back. Shopkeepers tend piles of objects—sticks, flowers, acorns, perhaps pieces of clay from out back by the swing set. Some sell actual food. They will spend the next day or week selling or trading things, opening for business when they arrive in the morning shadows and playing until late afternoon sun clears the oaks. Some will form partnerships; others will go it alone. The town will form contours of relationship, aesthetics, and justice, growing as the game grows. Then one day, rainwater washes the chalk down the driveway. The game drifts away like the flowers, only to return another day or year, whenever the players bring it back.

One day some years ago I passed two students walking and talking across campus. The first said, "And then you see a door."

"I try to open it," says the second.

"It's locked."

"I look for a key."

They pass by, consumed by their game. Dungeons and Dragons fans will recognize the exchange, and indeed Fairhaven's beloved Paper Game has its roots in the role-playing game known as D&D (itself a very popular pastime on campus.) But these two had no books, no dice, and no maps. Their particular variant occurred in real time. The Dungeon Master created the story and the world as he went along, leading his partner right along with his imagination.

What's become known as the Paper Game at Fairhaven started when some D&D folks began drawing, on paper, their own worlds to explore. As with D&D, players spend hours upon hours in these worlds, developing a unique cadence to their speech, and a deep connection. Some, like the two I encountered, took the Paper Game beyond even the paper, no longer wanting to be tied to a table or anything two-dimensional at all. Some girls have recently brought the Paper Game back to the paper, hybridizing it again by adding a paper doll component to their created worlds.

The Paper Game represents a prime example of what Fairhaveners do when they play. They create worlds, both large and small. They lose themselves in the game, sometimes forgetting to eat as they play. They play with language and culture. They discover situations and deal with them. They form deep partnerships. They evolve the game itself to suit their needs.

After ten years of instinctive recognition that free play is essential to healthy development in young people, now we have research to confirm its value. Chasing each other across campus, playing pirates or puppies? According to social scientists, free play is vital for cognitive and emotional development. From a recent story about the research:

It turns out that all that time spent playing make-believe actually helped children develop a critical cognitive skill called executive function. Executive function has a number of different elements, but a central one is the ability to self-regulate. Kids with good self-regulation are able to control their emotions and behavior, resist impulses, and exert self-control and discipline.

Poor executive function is associated with high dropout rates, drug use and crime. In fact, good executive function is a better predictor of success in school than a child's IQ. Children who are able to manage their feelings and pay attention are better able to learn. As executive function researcher Laura Berk explains, "Self-regulation predicts effective development in virtually every domain."[10] Researchers say "private speech" is the catalyst for development in free play.

According to Berk, one reason make-believe is such a powerful tool for building self-discipline is because during make-believe, children engage in what's called private speech: they talk to themselves about what they are going to do and how they are going to do it.

For many of our younger students, playing good old-fashioned House is one of the games that generates this self-talk. Who's the mom? How would she act? Who's the dad? Has he just come home from work? Do they have pets? What's the situation, and how will it unfold? House games proceed for hours. Roles might solidify, sometimes lasting a whole year, or they may alternate. Regardless, the players are again creating a world, figuring out how to be by pretending. Variants have included animating Beanie Babies and American Girl dolls. Lately, students have been playing Webkinz and Littlest Pet Shops.

Maybe the most paradoxical game one might encounter at Fairhaven and other Sudbury campuses is the ever-popular School. It's unmistakable. The teacher stands at the head of the class, directing her seated students. When playing School, students tend to focus on the three R's. Often, the teacher is deliberately bossy and strict. She assigns homework and grades her pupils. "School" illustrates how anything is ripe for gaming at Fairhaven. The students know what their peers are doing in traditional school, and they want to know what it may be like. So they play it.

The phenomenon of playing games concretizes many of the best attributes a Fairhaven education offers. People who wish to play a game learn how to make things happen. Students choose their level of activity. Devoted participants can attain mastery. Age mixing accelerates the quality and density of the game, often blurring the lines between teachers and learners. Time often stands still for gamers. The best games seem to be at once fun and serious.

Connecting lessons of play to life lessons, the Duke of Wellington is said to have commented, "The Battle of Waterloo was won on the playing fields of Eton." Surely Fairhaven students will look back at their time playing Scientists and Monkeys, or basketball, or Capture the Flag, as some of their most enjoyable times at school.

Finally, the names of the games don't matter. As an observer, I can see that free people playing games are developing hosts of skills and experiencing whole categories of growth—strategy, mathematics, language, socialization, physical fitness, tactics, artistic sensibilities, and economics all come to mind. Yet the activity defies easy analysis . In the end, playing games embodies who we are, and it creates who we become. It advances our humanity unlike any other pastime.

A group of students crosses the breezeway between buildings. "We're going to play hide and seek in the new building. Want to come?"

I accept their invitation.

An Open Letter
To the Department of Education

December 26, 2007

To Whom It May Concern:

I read today in the Washington Post *that American students rank twenty-third among industrial nations in math test scores. The story documented aggressive strategies to combat the problem, including a federal task force, new graduate school programs for math educators, and teaching algebra concepts to children in kindergarten. If children are not algebra-savvy by third grade, it may be too late, experts advise with much seriousness. Should we fail, they continue, our workforce will suffer irreparable gaps in science and engineering. It's Sputnik redux.*

The five-year-olds at Fairhaven School spend their days playing—building forts, capturing the flag, role-playing in games like House. Our students learn math and algebra when they're ready. I picture thousands upon thousands of four and five-year-olds wrestling with algebra, all for the sake of harvesting a few more engineers, a handful more scientists. Whither creativity in people who are destined to become, not scientists, but actors, writers, firemen?

Presumably, also, we want our engineers and scientists to innovate. The opportunities abound—curing cancer, finding clean energy sources, exploring space. For every scientist found in the ever more rigorous mathematics teaching and testing regime, how many will we lose? For every kindergartener ready to sit still and do math, how many are unable? How many brilliant ideas will disappear altogether because of each hour of play lost to algebra? The latest research on cognitive and emotional development confirms what young people show us every day—free play produces healthier, smarter people than force-fed, outcome-based instruction.

In kindergarten, for goodness sake, let them play. The scientists will emerge. Einstein got it right when he said, "Everything that is really great and inspiring is created by the individual who can labor in freedom."

Ladies and gentlemen, the sky is falling yet again. Let the children play.

Respectfully,
Mark J. McCaig
Fairhaven School
Upper Marlboro, Maryland

Soup's On

The Kitchen Corporation is selling yesterday's soup in the new building kitchen.

This comes as an announcement, broadcast over the school's intercom. Then five minutes later, a more enticing update: The Kitchen Corp. is selling yesterday's soup, both chicken noodle and lentil, at half price. Come to the new building kitchen!

The day before, six or seven students and two staff members had filled the same kitchen with industry—chopping vegetables, plucking cooked chicken, kneading biscuits. The smell of sautéed onions and bread baking was irresistible, even downstairs. If you weren't a Corp. member, you could watch, but you had to stay out of the way. When the soup was on, they announced the news, although most of the customers didn't need any more sensory input.

We sat in the Chesapeake Room at a few tables. Classical music piped from a disc player across the room. Waiters took our orders back to the Dutch doors where the kitchen crew passed out the steaming bowls and biscuits. Service was prompt if a little bumpy. Cash pressed from our palms to the servers. Some of my fellow diners signed IOUs to the Kitchen Corporation. The lunch was hot and hearty, perfect for a crisp November day.

One fellow at my table complained that the chicken noodle was too salty, that the biscuits were too flat. People chided him. "What do you expect for three dollars?" asked one girl sopping the last of her soup with a biscuit.

"I expect better food," he said, undeterred.

"He can complain," I said in his defense. "Go tell the Kitchen Corp. Or just don't buy any next time. The customer is always right." He left the table and told one of the cooks, who promised to take it to the next Kitchen Corp. meeting that Friday.

Food. Feedback. Fairhaven.

Some Thoughts on Assessment

*All assessment is a hazard to learning, by subtly changing
the inner guidance of the activity to an organizing for outer rewards.*

—William Stafford

At Fairhaven

ONE OF THE FUNDAMENTAL PRINCIPLES of Fairhaven School
and its sister Sudbury schools is its embrace of an educational
process unfettered by class rank, grades, and standardized tests.
To a large degree, we agree with poet and writing teacher Stafford's observation, and our agreement has taken shape in the
lives of the young people growing up on campus. They pursue
activities because they want to do so, and so create themselves.
The only assessments in our setting are internal, parental, real

world or the direct result of the democratic process at school.

The bedrock of trust at Fairhaven is the foundation upon which students operate. Free to pursue interests and activities as they arise, our students develop accurate inner guidance systems. They become free agents in the Fairhaven ecosystem, coexisting and interacting with the rest of the people and their myriad chosen pursuits. Their assessment occurs in real time, because they decide what comes next.

People occasionally express concern that a Sudbury education is too child-centered, that it spoils students. Were self-assessment the only measurement at school, this concern would resonate. Critics should bear in mind that Fairhaven is an open, democratic community, where people express opinions—evaluative opinions—all the time.

Fairhaven's courageous parents assess our students. Initially they decide how their child would adapt to Fairhaven's combination of freedom and responsibility. Then, during the visiting week prior to admission, they observe their child. They ask questions (most parents whose children visit identify immediate, positive changes). Following enrollment, parents broaden their assessment sample to include their son's new friends. Fairhaven students develop friendships inside school as well as outside, and these often become deeper, in part because they're not devoting their evenings to homework. New criteria for measurement emerge: Is my child happy? Does he want to go to school? Is he communicating with me? Has he become more independent? Each family develops a new way to decide if their child is thriving. Sometimes they consult the staff at school informally or by arranging a conference.

In the sophisticated environment of the school, peers also offer constant informal assessment. Most days a visitor will find teenagers engaged in lengthy conversations on the porch, in the

lounge, perhaps in the Chesapeake Room. These sessions provide many levels of experience for our students—exchange of
information and knowledge, problem-solving think tanks, and
social skills refinement. Unlike the notorious cliques of other settings, egalitarianism and acceptance characterize these ongoing
groups. Still, peers are direct with feedback when someone is
full of it. Your friends and your acquaintances at Fairhaven will
let you know how you're doing, either directly through conversation or indirectly. A new, younger student who had been
obnoxious with his peers once came howling into the office. He
was complaining about another student not allowing him to
play with this other student's (very cool) Bionicle toys. I offered
to accompany him to the room where the others were playing.
The owner of the toys told me that the upset student can't use
his toys, "because he's not nice." At the time, it was true.

As full participants in the democratic processes at school,
students often make their assessments by debate and vote. The
Judicial Committee is a daily exercise in this evaluative process.
Did so-and-so break the rule? Is this other student a reliable
witness? Whose testimony is most compelling? Does he have a
history of integrity? They know the answers to these and other
questions about each student's character, and they apply them
to each decision. Sometimes students will be harsher with fellow students than soft-hearted staff. Because the staff members
do not prescribe opinions and we do not correct each and every
social interaction, students develop quite sophisticated people
skills, often through trial and error.

Staff members at Fairhaven School do, however, provide another layer of assessment. Among the many functions of the staff
on campus, we are paid, indeed hired, by the School Meeting to
express opinions throughout the day at school. Staff members
who completely avoid assessment are not doing their jobs.

Of course staff members only get hired if they recognize the value of all student pursuits. This does not trump honest assessment. Say an older student declares her desire to become a veterinarian. If a staff member hears this goal yet has seen no preparation for the general and specific requirements to make it happen, be it independent academic study, working with animals, or taking classes, he may express his honest opinion about her preparation. In a sense, he will assess her. Perhaps the student will reply that she plans to begin her study next year or after she leaves Fairhaven, perhaps she'll tell the adult to butt out. The point is that adults at Fairhaven add an important set of voices to the network of feedback.

The ultimate piece of assessment comes for students who seek a Fairhaven diploma. For most of the school's history, the Assembly (consisting of staff, students, parents, and elected public members) has listened to thesis defenses, then voted whether to award a diploma based upon the defense and the student's attendance and JC records. In the fall of 2006, the Assembly voted to hire three staff members from other Sudbury schools to hear and vote upon thesis defenses. With the support of the graduating class, who wanted their thesis defenses to be more challenging, we voted to raise the assessment bar higher.

The Mismeasure of Children

In his classic critique of western scientific quantification of intelligence, *The Mismeasure of Man*, paleontologist Stephen Jay Gould writes about "the abstraction of intelligence as a single entity, its location within the brain, its quantification as one number for each individual, and the use of these numbers to rank people in a single series of worthiness, invariably to find that oppressed and disadvantaged groups—races, classes, or sexes—are innately inferior and deserve their status."[11]

The temptation to reduce intelligence and achievement to mere numbers dies hard, as evidenced by the infamous study *The Bell Curve* in 1996. Fairhaven School has coexisted with another manifestation, the No Child Left Behind Federal education accountability law enacted in 2001 during the George W. Bush administration.

The hyper-testing environment mainstream education has become can trace its roots to one Sir Francis Galton, Charles Darwin's cousin. After reading Darwin's *Origin of Species*, Galton fathered the "eugenics" movement, coining the word after considering the term "viriculture." His hypothesis was simple and logical: "To give to the more suitable races or strains of blood a better chance of prevailing speedily over the less suitable than they otherwise would have had."

Infamously, Nazi Germany adopted policies of state eugenics, exterminating millions of undesirables, including Jews, homosexuals, the disabled, and the "feeble-minded" in hopes of breeding a genetically superior race. Not so famously, the Germans were adopting and accelerating North American eugenics practices. Between 1907 and 1963, 64,000 Americans who may have been "epileptic, imbecile, or feeble-minded" were sterilized in the United States, led by California. At the Nuremberg trials, the Nazis cited the American program as its inspiration. A patriotic poster championing American eugenics over Nazi eugenics says it all: "They're beating us at our own game."

Alberta, Canada pursued a notably aggressive policy, establishing a Eugenics Board to identify so-called imbeciles for sterilization. This Board administered the Stanford-Binet test to assess IQs. Many of those sterilized were immigrants learning English as a second language, whose intelligence was probably quite normal. [12]

This is the foundation upon which the specious notion

that we can measure intelligence and test our way out of an outdated educational system rests. The No Child Left Behind Act requires annual testing in reading and math, tying federal funds to successful school-wide test score improvements. Further, NCLB mandates removal of principals and teachers whose students do not meet standards.

While today's tests are not used to justify sterilization or to breed a superior race, they do serve to validate and entrench a misguided system. At precisely the time when educators should be innovating and adapting to the information age, the testing imperatives require, even threaten teachers not to innovate. Teachers teach to the tests. Test-taking skills supplant education. Rather than sterilize the people, NCLB and other previous attempts to fix our educational system can sterilize the infinite process we call education.

Casualties in this reductive approach include recess, the arts, and computer exploration. According to friends teaching in the system, the steady march of curriculum requirements day-to-day is towards dis-empowerment of teachers and students. There is no time for pedagogical inventiveness or creativity. It's all about the tests. No computer time? No arts? No play? What kind of society do we want to become?

Although the commentators and the politicians delight in the actual name "No Child Left Behind," perhaps its name reveals its most fatal flaw. Consider its very grammar. No child left behind by whom? Children are absolutely passive in the conventional mindset, where education has remained a process of politicians and educators dragging their clients where they will. Can we expect this process to produce leaders from those who have only been led? Thinkers who are often not allowed to think? Can we expect to see innovators emerge from a process that opposes innovation?

Pundits observe that the biggest problem with No Child Left Behind is its rhetorical brilliance. Which politician will propose, or even vote in favor of leaving children behind? Bound by self-preservation, elected officials seem reluctant to even begin the conversation about how we learn best, much less stop all the testing. Deadlines pass and standards remain unmet—children are being "left behind" by the accepted metrics—yet the proverbial heads are not rolling. Educational experts decry one hundred percent success as unrealistic; politicians are floating eighty-five percent trial balloons. The failing teachers are being retained in an alarming but predictable analogy to promoting failing students. The situation would be laughable were it not affecting so many lives.

Were any actual students ever interviewed or even asked what they think about the boondoggle? What do they want from their education? How do they want to prepare for an economy and a life, that are, by the way, quite different from the economies and lives the school system was originally designed to support? Where are their voices? The most onerous "leaving behind" has nothing to do with test results. Rather, it is the baseline ignoring of what students might even want to study, much less whom they may want to become.

Sudbury schools like Fairhaven articulate an educational model that fits today's needs. Student opinions matter at School Meeting; parent opinions matter at the Assembly. Fairhaven School is a place where each student is responsible for not just his school, but also for his own growth and education. Standardized tests are anathema in this setting.

How do you measure the growth of a rainbow? After how long has it achieved its maximum rainbowness? Are its colors in proper sequence? What's that inverted second rainbow, a rainbow disability? At Fairhaven, it's just another rainbow.

FHS Haiku

What she learned today
flew from blossom to blossom-
bright yellow swallowtail.

We debate sharp points.
Three scarlet leaves descending-
nature's neutrality.

Barefoot girl bending
Spies yesterday's green bud-
Unfurled miracle.

February's wet cold
ossifies moods, attitudes.
JC windows steam.

Some Field Trips from the First Ten Years

Folger Theater Shakespeare plays, two per year
Baltimore Aquarium
Apple picking
Washington Nationals baseball game
Various museums
Baltimore Zoo
Sugarloaf Mountain
Seven Springs Ski resort (overnight)
Catoctin State Park (overnight)
Cape Henlopen State Park (overnight)
Horseback riding
Ice skating
Grocery stores
Canoeing on the Patuxent River
Hiking the Billy Goat trail overlooking the Potomac River
Various plays
Movies
Feeding the homeless at the Lighthouse Shelter
Various working farms
Tree planting on the Patuxent River
Frisbee golf course
Washington Wizards games

Leaving Fairhaven

The "Real World" Question

ONE OF THE MOST COMMON CONCERNS we've heard from families interested in Fairhaven School is "Sure this sounds great, but what about the real world? How will Jenny do when she leaves Fairhaven?" Variants of this question have included the following: Will my child succeed in the real world? Can a Fairhaven School student successfully transfer to a traditional school? What does a Fairhaven diploma mean?

The first question presupposes, of course, that Fairhaven is not the real world. Visitors and Assembly members alike have adopted this rhetorical position since before we opened, and I'd like to address this premise first.

Arrive at Fairhaven and you do feel transported to an exotic oasis of freedom, student rights, and democratic practice. We are a haven from the compulsions and tyranny of contemporary schooling. Thus, proponents of the not-the-real-world argument have defined Fairhaven as a utopian fantasy, impractical for actual preparation for life in twenty-first century America.

Students at Fairhaven do one thing more than any other—they decide. Entrusted with complete responsibility for their education, young people here decide all day what to do, with whom to do it, where to do it, and for how long. Shall I skateboard or talk with my friends? Do math or check e-mail? Each day presents a full menu of decisions to make, and the enormous array of choices and results Fairhaven students experience is our golden formula for preparing for the world.

Put yourself in these shoes for a moment. You've arrived at school, and you've recorded your time of arrival on the attendance sheet. For the rest of your school day, you decide, and you live with the consequences of each decision. Let's say you go to the Art Room. Sit alone or with your buddies? Alone. Would you like to draw animé characters or throw a pot? Animé. Which colors? Green and blue, with blond hair. Of course our students navigate these options seamlessly and learn from them. Feedback is real and constant. Now multiply this process over twelve years; this is a Fairhaven curriculum.

A giant annual decision our students make is electing the staff for the following year. When a Fairhaven student votes whether or not to hire my colleagues and me, she joins a collective decision as to who goes and who stays, and for how long. Who does she want as role models, workers, teachers and friends? Who does she think will do well at helping to keep the school running?

Contact with the elected staff represents another aspect of Fairhaven students' participation in the real world. Our students can access our knowledge, our personalities, our life experiences, our labor, and our belief systems every day. Sometimes they get all of this in one School Meeting debate! We staff members argue, teach, and hang out throughout the school every day, elected elders for students to encounter.

In the fall of Fairhaven's first year, the School Meeting elected a teenager to serve on the Bookkeeping Committee alongside a colleague and myself. We met frequently, early in the year, to delegate tasks and create procedures, deciding that the student would pay the bills. She became a seventeen-year-old student bookkeeper, responsible for real financial jobs and decisions in a growing non-profit organization. She also became the first in an ongoing line of students who've worked for the school. Now the Theater Corporation has elected its first Treasurer, a student who will manage the Corp.'s finances from the Bookkeeping software in the office.

We've also elected and hired students as co-Attendance Clerk, School Meeting Chair and Secretary, Office Assistant, and cleaning personnel. In these roles they've worked for and alongside adults, always making real decisions and contributing actual labor. They've applied for positions, received performance evaluations and subsequent raises, and they've occasionally been let go. Both for them and their fellow students, their public work experience at school affords ongoing contact with the working world.

One of the most consistent points proponents of the "real world" argument make is that in jobs or college you often cannot choose your activity. Of course our students know this. Most of our students learn to follow orders in their families, or in jobs as teenagers, or on Cleaning Committee, or in doing some kind of mandatory community service for breaking a rule. Doing what you're told to do by the boss is really a simple thing to learn, one that Fairhaven students accomplish every day. They do, however, seem to have an ongoing willingness to question whether working in an especially harsh circumstance is worth the money. This seems a useful skill, one that I expect will manifest in later years as more of our young people establish entrepreneurial careers where they dictate the terms of their labor.[13]

Most students excel when elected or hired by School Meeting, and therein model excellence for all to see. However, some do not excel, and witnessing poor work and then having to deal with it educates our students equally about the world. Can we work with him a little longer, giving him a chance to shape up? Or do we have to fire him now? Presented with a variety of student workers, fellow students wrestle with an equal variety of questions and conclusions about this work.

We conclude such debates in School Meeting, another rich entry point for Fairhaven students into the real world. It's where we decide all the details of running the school, from admissions policy to zoo field trips and everything in between. Students participate in and observe substantive decision-making with students and staff weekly. Is having a skateboarding half-pipe worth the additional liability for the school? What color should we paint the student lounge? Should we hire the dance teacher for another eight weeks?

School Meeting discussions must be civil and must follow parliamentary procedures, a system involving motions, amendments and lots of discussion and voting. It is similar to *Robert's Rules of Order*.[14] The process empowers students more than anything else I've seen in my decades of experience in education. Eight-year-olds debate sixty-year-olds, sometimes carrying the day. Impassioned voting blocs descend upon the meeting, encountering a variety of opinions and dealing with them in a polite manner.

Let me be clear about School Meeting: since it's a weekly meeting charged with deciding all the minute details of running a school, it can be tedious! Although some of our young people participate in every School Meeting, many choose other activities, entrusting the weekly decisions to others.

Every year at least once I have a version of the following conversation:

Me: Your bike has to be stored under the stairs.
Student: Well, I didn't know that was a rule!
Me: School Meeting just voted on it last week.
Student: Nobody told me.
Me: Here, let me show you in the minutes.

I'll show her the posted minutes, right beside the agenda for the next week's meeting. I may tell her that I'd like to hear her opinion in the meeting and remind her that it's every Wednesday at one o'clock in the Chesapeake Room. As a citizen of our small democracy, she has the right to speak out and vote for what she thinks is right. Every student quickly learns that those who don't take part don't have a say in what happens. But they can, at any point, decide to get involved. How "real" is that?

An island of freedom and student rights? Perhaps. Yet Fairhaven School is at the same time an island with rules and responsibilities, held together by a transparent, democratic system of governance. It's a place with real consequences for actions and for inactions. We think combining freedom and rights in a true democracy is the best of all possible preparations for joining civil society.

Re-entry

Since the first year, some Fairhaven students have left prior to graduation. Sometimes their families have moved—to California, Tennessee, maybe to Florida. Sometimes the students themselves choose to go to what they call "regular school." They may want more people their age. Maybe they want to play high school sports (aside from the year of the Cougars basketball team, we haven't had the number of players necessary to field a team). Sometimes parents' attitudes about schooling shift, and they choose to return their child to the educational mainstream. Tuition may become too much of a hardship for a family. Often, families that leave cite combinations of reasons.

So we have accumulated ten years of anecdotal information on one of the consistent, reasonable concerns about Sudbury schooling: what if a student has to return to mainstream schooling? I cannot overstate the answer—not only do our students who leave before graduating do fine, but Fairhaven students excel when they enter compulsory schools.

For students of education like me, this presents a fascinating set of questions, one that bears more investigation in a later publication. For now, I'll make some brief observations as to how in the world students who come from a non-compulsory setting quickly join the honor roll in a compulsory setting. What gives?

Many families who choose Fairhaven seem to be think-out-side-the-box families. They are willing to trust their children on a deep level, and years at Fairhaven have reinforced the independence of the young people. According to some alumni, going inside-the-box of a tradition school has been easy in comparison to Fairhaven. Less interesting, perhaps, less exciting, but pretty easy.

To be sure, some students have crammed some of the academic basics prior to enrolling in compulsory schools. Many were, in fact, re-enrolling after a comparatively short time at Fairhaven. Some parents (those whose attitudes about educational philosophy had shifted) hired tutors. Yet none of even these students had anything approaching the comprehensive workload of compulsory curricula.

One conclusion is that, just as the child in the fairy tale finally observed, the emperor actually wears no clothes! The notion that one needs to sit in class all day and do homework for much of the night, for years on end, is spurious, even in order to excel in a traditional curriculum. Children can and do learn academic subjects quickly—if they want to.

Other answers to our former students' startling rate of success must come from their Fairhaven experience. First, as written elsewhere, they are completely at ease with adults. I asked one student how his first year of middle school was going. "Everything's been great," he said. "Algebra's tough, but I just talk to the teacher after class. It's getting easier." Fairhaven students communicate at an honest and sophisticated level. Years of talking with peers, younger students, older students, and staff members have prepared them for whatever comes next in their lives, including a compulsory school setting.

Another former student said, "I just figure out what the teacher wants, and do it. It's sort of a game, I guess." Years of playing games and figuring out what people want was precisely what she had done at Fairhaven. For her, public school was just a big game, and she was winning.

In the end, it seems that the salutary effects of trust and freedom buttressed by responsibility prepare our students for traditional school. Years of hanging out, talking, and playing have, indeed, prepared them. They enter other educational settings with an intangible confidence. They know what they have to do, and they do it.

Charlie returned as a visitor a month into his first year at middle school. Leaving was not his choice. "How's it going?" I asked.

"It's fine," he replied, flat. He'd grown several inches since our exit interview the previous spring, as had his curly shock of hair.

"His lowest grade is a 'C'." said one of his Fairhaven buddies with pride.

"You remember? I told you middle school would be easy for a smart guy like you," I offered, always on thin ice when discussing compulsory schooling with students in the system. He knows what I think about the rigmarole, but I want to support him. "You're always welcome here," I said, shaking Charlie's hand, perfectly aware that he could interpret my remark as a one-day greeting or as an enticement to return. I left him to his visiting day, wondering how a drink from this familiar cup of freedom would taste.

We keep in touch with those who leave, allow them visits as best we can. Relationships at Fairhaven become very close, life-long bonds. Still, as a staff, we must embody tolerance for each student's educational path, even when their education continues elsewhere.

If it were up to us, however, every Charlie would stay. Although three years of freedom is adequate preparation for middle school, it pales in comparison to six years at Fairhaven, or twelve. Remember, our premise is that the emperor that is mainstream schooling is, at best, scantily clad. Come to a Fairhaven graduation if you'd like to see and hear the resplendent outfits our graduates wear when they leave.

The Diploma Process

Perhaps no subject has undergone more debate at Sudbury schools than the diploma process. At issue is a fundamental philosophical contradiction: in a setting where all activities are valued as educational, how can we evaluate those choices and award a diploma? At the same time, the word "diploma" means something in the larger society, so how can we award a diploma without some evaluative component? Fairhaven's first decade has included a few diploma processes, and these were informed by the procedures adopted by Sudbury Valley School.

One might wonder why we have a diploma at all. Some might say that from a school philosophy perspective, offering no diploma has the most purity. Indeed, some students have chosen to leave Fairhaven without diplomas, and their lives seem unburdened by this absence. From day one, the majority of our students have absolutely wanted to be able to leave, in fact to graduate, with a high school diploma in hand. For this reason, the Assembly (consisting of parents, staff members, and students) has always provided a means for older students to get a diploma.

The concept for acquiring a diploma was devised by the Sudbury Valley School Assembly before Fairhaven opened. Candidates for a diploma must be at least sixteen years old and must have attended the school for a number of years (at Fairhaven, like Sudbury Valley, it used to be two years and now it's three). The central job for a diploma candidate is to write and defend the thesis that they have prepared themselves to become effective adults in the larger community.

The Fairhaven School Assembly first voted to adopt a diploma process whereby the candidates defended their theses before the school Assembly. Most theses inventory a student's academic career, both at Fairhaven and elsewhere. A typical thesis also includes what the student's future plans include, and how he has prepared for them. The Assembly members received the final draft and prepared questions for each candidate. The final piece of the process became the thesis defenses, where each candidate fielded tough questions from parents, staff, and fellow students. Following the defense, the Assembly then voted by secret ballot whether the students had successfully defended the thesis and then whether to award that student a diploma.

In our second year the philosophical purists among the Assembly held the day, voting to enact a diploma process bereft of evaluation. Candidates who had met the minimum time of enrollment requirement received diplomas, no questions asked (literally). For a variety of reasons, including concern that we might secure the dreaded label of "diploma mill," the Assembly voted the following year to return to the thesis defense model.

Thesis defenses developed into rites of passage, evening events that were well attended. Younger students joined older community members by asking questions or heaping praise upon candidates. In a confluence of play and practice that is pure Fairhaven, each year younger students role-played thesis defenses on the day between the actual evening defenses. Graduates spoke well of the challenges and the stimulating dialogue provided by thesis defenses. Parents appreciated getting to know candidates by way of the thesis defense nights.

While on the one hand, the staff, students and parents praised students for developing their own educational path, the school community sometimes had to shed light on any troubling aspect of a candidate's thesis or history at school. Staff members and students became the messengers regarding poor attendance, JC issues, or disconnection between the candidates' written theses and their actual experience at school. They also challenged those whose theses seemed weak. Some thesis defenses became hopelessly schizophrenic affairs, on the one hand affirmative capstones to high school careers, on the other hand very public airings of school records. In addition, it became clear that the Assembly, as a body, was unable to vote down even the most problematic candidates. We were back to diploma mill.

Fortunately, a similar dynamic spurred the Assembly at Sudbury Valley School to modify this unique diploma process. Borrowing from the structure of thesis defenses at graduate schools, they voted to hire a committee of three staff members from other Sudbury schools to come to SVS each spring, replacing the Assembly as the voting body before which students defended their theses.

Going to Sudbury Valley to be on their inaugural Diploma Committee was my first professional trip as a Fairhaven staff member. Although I had attended several summer conferences there, I had never visited the school in order to perform a specific task. The SVS Records Clerk mailed me the fifteen theses and JC records prior to the trip. Reading them was fascinating, providing ample windows into both the students themselves and their school. I joined two colleagues from Sudbury schools in Florida and Washington state in the task of reading, hearing and evaluating theses from the SVS diploma candidates.

We spent three days interviewing the candidates in an upstairs corner room at SVS. We asked each student our prepared questions. Why are you taking a year off before college? How did serving as School Meeting Chair prepare you to become a responsible member of the larger community? If you don't make it as a professional golfer, what's your backup plan? It says here that School Meeting suspended you for an altercation with your girlfriend. Can you detail this episode? I met students who reminded me precisely of students at Fairhaven, seeming Sudbury archetypes—the honorable Dungeons and Dragons girl, the hyper-communicative and confident staff kid, the earnest boy who wants to work with his hands.

Each interview achieved a depth of inquiry that Assembly thesis defenses could never approach. Instead of being able to ask one or maybe two questions, each of the three Committee members asked as many as we wanted. Threads of discussion emerged and played out. By the end of each hour-long defense, we had a clear sense of who the young person across the table had become, and whether they had successfully defended their thesis.

A wonderful ancillary result for me was a renewed affirmation of the Sudbury model. These were, for the most part, impressive, articulate young people, exactly the kind of people we hope to send into the world. They were interesting and honest, artistic and realistic. They were assets to the larger community, and they came across as quite prepared for "the real world" beyond the bucolic campus of Sudbury Valley. The two students we voted down just seemed like they still had some growing up to do. In follow-up interviews, both the Committee members and the graduates agreed that this new procedure worked well.

In our ninth year, staff and students planning to graduate met early in the year to discuss changing the diploma process at the fall Assembly meeting. Of the ten students planning to graduate that spring, nine embraced the new procedure. They wanted the diploma to mean more; they wanted a more difficult challenge! They agreed that the Assembly vote had its merits, but that in the end it was too much of a home game. The prospect of writing a thesis, then defending it to three strangers appealed to them. With student support, the fall Assembly enacted the new policy.

Some Assembly members, however, expressed concerns about the Assembly losing the distinctive, public question-and-answer exchanges that characterized thesis defenses. Taking the recommendation of a subcommittee, the Assembly voted to hybridize the procedure, requiring each candidate to declare publicly his or her intent at a special winter Assembly meeting. They did so, and the Assembly continued its tradition of challenging and encouraging candidates before they graduate.

The first year of the new procedure was a smashing success. Students, staff members, and parents embraced the change. Because they were writing for strangers, students focused more energy on their written theses, energizing their thesis subcommittees like never before, writing and revising multiple drafts. Many candidates also used their thesis subcommittees to practice answering difficult questions prior to the committee's arrival.

As for members of the staff like myself, we were able for the first time to focus solely on supporting diploma candidates. We spent time helping them revise their theses in subcommittees, reassuring them about their readiness for the interviews, and helping them see who they had become. The Diploma Committee arrived from Sudbury Valley School in Massachusetts, Clearwater School in Washington, and Alpine Valley School in Colorado. Fairhaven crackled with excitement as they took over the Meeting Room and the Lounge for their work. Candidates dressed up, pacing the halls in anticipation. The rest of the school respected the need for quiet. The process was rigorous and stimulating for the students, just as they had hoped the previous September.

The Graduation Assembly had a special sheen that year, as we celebrated these first graduates under the new procedure. They had run the gauntlet of a Diploma Committee made up of strangers, and all seven of them had been awarded diplomas. Because we as an institution do not test or rank our students, subjective encounters—getting to know who our students turn out to be—have proven to be the best measure of a Fairhaven education. Both the diploma process and the graduation ceremony provide Assembly members this opportunity. Speakers praised them, detailing their individual virtues and achievements. Each graduate spoke, offering gratitude and a window into themselves. A central theme was their readiness for the larger community as they headed off to various higher education institutes and jobs, joining the growing crowd of people who leave Fairhaven uniquely prepared for whatever comes next.

Why a Fairhaven education? What outcomes can parents expect from their children in this environment? Although each student's experiences differ, definite patterns have emerged in our first decade. Common attributes of a Fairhaven-educated person include the following:

- She is a high-level communicator, able to express herself in private and in public with clarity, whether she's speaking with a five-year-old or an adult she's meeting for the first time.
- He has thought long and hard about learning and education. He knows how he best learns.
- She has a code of ethics. She knows the rules and she has a keen sense of fairness.
- He is at ease with himself.
- She can move from one activity to the next. She is comfortable with new situations. She is independent.
- He enjoys the outdoors and its natural systems.
- She is computer literate.

• He can respond to his life in a creative manner, and he has an evolving personal aesthetic.

• She knows what she wants in life, and she is willing to work to get it.

This partial list suggests only patterns; each student's tendencies differ. As the school becomes more established, so too do the attributes of our graduates. A future project will be to study in depth the young people who leave Fairhaven School. Until then, based upon both our considerable contact with our former students and the data from Sudbury Valley's research on its graduates, we assert that people leaving Fairhaven will succeed in the world.

Fairhaven alumni have been accepted to a number of colleges, universities, and other institutions of higher learning, including:

Academy of Art University, San Francisco
Beacon University
Brooklyn College
Champlain College
DePaul University
DigiPen Institute of Technology
Fashion Institute of Design and Merchandising
Goucher College
Guilford College
Hampshire College
Hocking College
Hollins University
Manhattanville College
Mary Baldwin College
Morgan State University
New College of Florida
Pennsylvania State University
Prescott College
Ringling College of Art and Design
St. John's College
St. Mary's College of Maryland
Sarah Lawrence College
Savannah College of Art and Design
School of the Art Institute of Chicago
School of the Museum of Fine Arts
Temple University
The New School
Towson University
University of Maryland, Baltimore County
University of Maryland, College Park
University of North Carolina
Ursinis College
Video Symphony TV and Post-Production Institute
Washington College

The Wise Silence

A note of music gains significance from the silence on either side.
—Anne Morrow Lindbergh

EACH SUDBURY SCHOOL pulsates with language. Conversations pepper the hallways and the rooms, the porches and the woods. As other chapters attest, the School Meeting and the Judicial Committee operate at a very high linguistic level. People in these meetings defend themselves and their positions. They try to persuade with words. Often multiple threads of language unspool in the same room. I assert that Fairhaven School is, in fact, a communication factory, and that our people can talk with almost any person, about almost anything.

Nevertheless, most of the tours I conduct every other Friday also pass one or more students immersed in silence. She may be sitting alone on the porch, rocking. Or he may be in a room, alone. Perhaps two students occupy a couch, and the only sound they're making is the clicking of their knitting needles. This chapter will briefly explore the essential phenomena of silence, quiet, and solitude at Fairhaven School.

We always hope that the school represents a continuum of human experience, "its own little world" as a new student remarked when he first visited. From the start, then, we have accommodated the more quiet students in our loud, sometimes argumentative milieu. Since the Sudbury philosophy is so accepting, we tend to attract people open to differences not just in learning styles but also in ways of being. Some folks are just quieter, and Fairhaven accepts them as such.

Even when we had just one building, the School Meeting has always voted to designate at least one room a Quiet Room. A few years ago, when we opened our second building, we reserved one room for silence. It was the only place on campus where absolutely no talking was allowed, and JC restricted anyone from it who was charged with breaking this rule. Recently School Meeting changed the Silent Room to a Quiet Room in which whispering is allowed. The rules designating silent rooms and quiet rooms face periodic challenges from the floor of School Meeting, when advocates for a louder use decry the inefficiency of the quieter rooms. It is a testament to the determination of the quieter students that no matter how vocal the talkative students are, School Meeting has persisted in providing at least one oasis of quiet in the school.

Often a quieter student needs some time to get used to the very different environment that is a Sudbury school. While some new arrivals dive right into the verbal mix, many hang back. They listen; they watch. Remember, new students have no course of study laid before them. In many ways, the other people on campus are their course of study. Initial silence makes sense as new students assess the school culture and the personalities of scores of staff and students. Staff members have learned to check in with new students, but also to allow them the luxury of a very quiet beginning if they choose it. Most of these quieter arrivals ease one day into the rushing verbal tide, each at precisely their own pace and comfort level.

A Fairhaven education allows for prodigious exercise in thought, and every quiet student represents one way of realizing this potential. Of course people who are quiet are still thinking. They are forming ideas; their synapses are firing. Our students develop sharp people skills, in part from quiet, close observation of their peers. Like them, I'll sometimes sit in the Circle Room and soak in the passing humanity. It's always a revelation. As we have become a more sophisticated democratic community, the level of debate and communication at School Meeting rises. Once, after we had decided a contentious issue, I asked an older teen who was nearing the end of his second year at the school why he hadn't spoken. "School Meeting scares me," he replied with a sheepish grin. After nearly two years! So he listened to the heated decision-making in silence, and he raised his hand to vote when it was time. Perhaps he will join the debate in his third or fourth year, exactly when he is ready to break his particular School Meeting silence.

What about the occasional student who occupies the far end of the quiet spectrum? He may only respond when someone else initiates the conversation. Perhaps he will make the Quiet Room his home, so enamored of quiet is he. School Meeting members may discuss his use of the school, and check in with him from time to time. In the end, he becomes like the nine-year-old who doesn't yet read or the nineteen-year-old who doesn't drive. Trusting people's schedules and choices is our starting point. So long as he communicates as needed by JC and

School Meeting, and so long as he follows the school's rules, his silence must be considered golden.

Free from another's idea of how she should fill her days, a Fairhaven student lives the actual contours of her life at school. Sometimes this includes crises. A caring community, we tend to sense these times and reach out to communicate. Often, the student wants a listener, and she will pour out her heart. Other times, she will want the opposite. More than once I've heard a loud and clear, "Leave me alone" or " I don't want to talk about it." Not merely a personality style or a way to get used to Fairhaven, silence is a right. Even in the Judicial Committee, which relies on testimony to investigate cases, defendants may "plead the Fifth" to not incriminate themselves. Although in JC this is a rare occurrence, people at the school indeed have the right to remain silent.

Silence's physical cousin is solitude. Fairhaven is a complex social entity, stratified like a living geologic field. Some people have a very small, tight crew; others navigate various crowds, going from the gamers to the skateboarders to the Munchkins all in one day. Solitude is another option. For some, being alone may be a daily choice, at least for part of the day. For others, being alone may only transpire once or twice a year. Regardless, we can only speculate how important those walks by the stream, those times swinging alone in the backyard, or those fifteen minutes sitting in a quiet room are to the growth and development of our students.

Transcendentalist philosopher Ralph Waldo Emerson named times like these and this essential aspect of the human spectrum "the wise silence." For many students, this silence is like the dark side of the moon. Silence enables the verbal acuity and the communication fireworks that later will become the bright, public face of their Fairhaven education.

Goodbye

Zane, a graduate of Fairhaven, used to pop into each room before going home at day's end to say goodbye to each fellow student. Some days I reprise his practice.

To the girl in the shop painting the last bit of gold on her plaster dinosaur head, the one she plans to place atop her family's Christmas tree, goodbye. To the crowded table of people drawing in the Art Room. To the three teenagers talking and doing the Washington Post crossword, as they do every day, goodbye.

To the boys waging a Dungeons and Dragons campaign in the room they proudly named The Chamber of Nerds, although they do not seem to hear me, goodbye. To the boys passing, in between rounds of hide and seek. To the girls chatting online in the brick-floored Sonora Room, good afternoon. To the teenagers emptying trash cans, vacuuming, or mopping, a goodbye and keep up the good work. To the trio sharing a late afternoon pizza, one of whom's on her pink cell phone, as usual, goodbye.

In another room, a hearty farewell to the boys engaged in the latest massively multiplayer online role-playing game (MMORPG.) To the new girl and her pals sitting on the porch and in its rafters. To a colleague passing between buildings, see you tomorrow. To the helmeted boys biking around the driveway circle, then bombing down the hill, a shouted goodbye. To the girl some twenty feet up an oak tree, a wave.

To the cluster of teenagers knitting and crocheting around a table, answering the day's questions, considering the school's current issues, *poking fun at me, goodbye. To the girls playing chase in the Chesa-peake Room, slow down and goodbye. To the guys in the kitchen hav-ing a late lunch. To the teenager signing out for the day while I wait my turn to sign out as well, adios.*

To the young man drumming in the music room, a nod through the window. To the girl drawing by way of a tablet onto a computer screen, wow, that's amazing, and goodbye. To the four students in another computer room, a quiet goodbye. To the young girls arrang-ing a play date, crowding around the hallway telephone, a touch on the shoulder. Goodbye to the girls voting with their American Girl dolls by raising the dolls' hands, as in all in favor of this doll joining our doll club? To the house players under the stage in the Kid Nook, whoever they are, goodbye as well.

To another colleague sorting and shelving books in the Lounge. To the teenagers planning to come in the next day with shaved heads, good luck with that, and goodbye. To the girl in the Quiet Room, read-ing in a wingback chair, a whispered goodbye when she looks up from her novel. To the teenager researching colleges and culinary schools on the computer next to her, an informal salute.

To them all, a grateful goodbye and a heartfelt thanks for yet an-other day among thousands as we build this school one idea at a time, decision by decision, action to action, blessed life by life.

Notes

PAGE	NOTE	
21	1	*the function of a child is to live his own life...* A.S. Neill, *Summerhill,* Wikipedia, Summerhill entry. Available at: http://en.wikipedia.org/wiki/Summerhill_School.
22	2	Greenberg, Daniel, *Free At Last* (Framingham, Mass.: The Sudbury Valley School Press, 1987).
26	3	*The Creed of the Fairhaven Community Fellowship* is its primary document, plan and charter. It describes the spiritual and philosophical principles to which all Fellowship business and activities must conform. The Creed of the Fellowship is as follows: "We believe in the free and responsible search for personal truth and meaning. We believe in the inherent worth and dignity of every human being. We believe in the formation of a spiritual organization that embraces diversity of thought and belief while providing for its membership a supportive and stimulating community. We believe in providing for our children, as well as for ourselves, a democratically self-governed educational environment within which they are free to explore life in all its complexity."
71	4	Louv, Richard, *Last Child in the Woods* (Chapel Hill, NC: Algonquin Books, 2005).
78	5	*her ongoing education about relationships...* See Hanna Greenberg's "The Evil of the Teachable Moment" in *The Sudbury Valley School Experience* (Framingham, Mass.: The Sudbury Valley School Press, 1992).

PAGE	NOTE	
78	6	*To suggest that ecoschools...* Louv, 218.
79	7	Berry, Wendell from "On the Hill Late at Night," *Collected Poems 1957-1982* (Albany, CA: North Point Press, 1987).
80	8	Rogers, Pattiann from "Knot" in *Firekeeper* (Minneapolis: Milkweed Editions, 1994).
126	9	*Blowback*: Dictionary.com. *Webster's New Millennium TM Dictionary of English*, Preview Edition (v 0.9.7). Lexico Publishing Group, LLC. Available at: http://dictionary.reference.com/browse/blowback.
136	10	*Self-regulation predicts effective development...* Laura Berk, executive function researcher, quoted in Alix, Spiegel, "Old-Fashioned Play Builds Serious Skills." Available at: http://www.npr.org/templates/story/story.php?storyId=19212514.
144	11	Stephen Jay Gould, *The Mismeasure of Man* (New York: Norton & Co., 1981), 24-25.
145	12	*to give to the more suitable races...* Francis Galton, *Inquiries into human faculty and its development.* (London, Macmillan, 1883): 17, fn1. Available at: http://en.wikipedia.org/wiki/Eugenics.
153	13	See Daniel Greenberg, Mimsy Sadofsky and Jason Lempka, *The Pursuit of Happiness* (Framingham, Mass.: The Sudbury Valley School Press, 2005).
153	14	We use Alice Sturgis, *Standard Code of Parliamentary Procedure* (New York: McGraw-Hill, 1988).

ABOUT THE AUTHOR

MARK MCCAIG has been a staff member at Fairhaven School since it opened. Before Fairhaven he taught in a variety of other settings, including public school, Catholic School, Montessori school, and outdoor education programs. Mark has degrees from the University of Maryland and Harvard University, and has been a contributing writer for *The Bay Weekly*. He lives on the shores of the Chesapeake Bay with his family.

Dejame Ramon
en paz. no me
acoses.
Merl.